REVISE

for MEI Structured Mathematics

Mathematics

$\phi + \dot{\phi}$

A

Series Editor
Charlie Stripp

Authors
Catherine Berry, Sophie Goldie, Richard Lissaman and Charlie Stripp

HODDER
EDUCATION
AN HACHETTE UK COMPANY

Every effort has been made to trace all copyright holders, but if any have been inadvertently overlooked the Publishers will be pleased to make the necessary arrangements at the first opportunity.

Although every effort has been made to ensure that website addresses are correct at time of going to press, Hodder Education cannot be held responsible for the content of any website mentioned in this book. It is sometimes possible to find a relocated web page by typing in the address of the home page for a website in the URL window of your browser.

Hachette UK's policy is to use papers that are natural, renewable and recyclable products and made from wood grown in sustainable forests. The logging and manufacturing processes are expected to conform to the environmental regulations of the country of origin.

Orders: please contact Bookpoint Ltd, 130 Milton Park, Abingdon, Oxon OX14 4SB.
Telephone: (44) 01235 827720. Fax: (44) 01235 400454. Lines are open 9.00 – 5.00, Monday to Saturday, with a 24-hour message answering service.
Visit our website at www.hoddereducation.co.uk

© Catherine Berry, Sophie Goldie, Richard Lissaman, Charlie Stripp, 2010
First published in 2010 by
Hodder Education,
An Hachette UK Company
338 Euston Road
London NW1 3BH

Impression number   5 4 3 2 1
Year   2013 2012 2011 2010

Dynamic Learning Student Online website © Catherine Berry, Sophie Goldie, Richard Lissaman, Charlie Stripp, 2010; with contributions from Louisa Mousley and Tom Carter; developed by Infuze Limited and MMT Limited; cast: Tom Frankland; recorded at Alchemy Soho.

Typeset in 11/12 Helvetica by Tech-Set Ltd., Gateshead, Tyne & Wear
Printed in India

A catalogue record for this title is available from the British Library

ISBN: 978 0 340 957387

Contents

Introduction

Welcome to this Revision Guide for the MEI Further Pure 1 unit!

The book is organised into 13 sections covering the various topics in the syllabus. A typical section is four pages long; the first three pages contain essential information and key worked examples covering the topic. At the start of each chapter, there are page references to where the section topics are covered in the textbook.

The last page in each section has questions for you to answer so that you can be sure that you have really understood the topic. There is a multiple-choice exercise and an exam-style question. If you are to gain the greatest possible benefit from the book, and so do your best in the FP1 exam, you should work through these for yourself and then refer to the accompanying website to check your answers.

The multiple-choice questions cover the basic ideas and techniques. It is really important that you work through them carefully; guessing will do you no good at all. When you have decided on the answer you think is right, enter it on the website. If you are right, it tells you so and gives the full solution; check that your answer wasn't just a fluke. If your choice is not right, the website gives you advice about your mistake; the possible wrong answers have all been designed to pick out particular common misunderstandings. The explanations on the website are based on the most likely mistakes; even if you make a different mistake, you will usually find enough help to set you on the right path so that you can try again.

When you come onto the exam-style question, write out your best possible answer. Then go to the website. You will find the solution displayed step-by-step, together with someone talking you through it and giving you helpful advice.

So the book contains the essential information to revise for the exam and, critically, also enables you to check that you have understood it properly. That is a recipe for success.

Finally, a word of warning. This book is designed to be used together with the textbook and not as a replacement for it. This Revision Guide will help you to prepare for the exam but to do really well you also need the deep understanding that comes from the detailed explanations you will find in the textbook.

Good learning and good luck!

Catherine Berry, Sophie Goldie, Richard Lissaman, Charlie Stripp

Where you see the following icon **⊃L**, please refer to the Dynamic Learning Student Online website. Information on how to access this website is printed on the inside front cover of the book.

Accompanying books
MEI Structured Mathematics FP1
ISBN 978 0 340 81460 4

Companion to Advanced Mathematics and Statistics
ISBN 978 0 340 95923 7

Matrices

Working with matrices

2, 6
28, 36
41, 42

A ABOUT THIS TOPIC

Matrices are important in many areas of mathematics, with wide applications in science, engineering and business. This section introduces matrices and looks at matrix addition, subtraction and multiplication.

R REMEMBER

- This topic is accessible directly from GCSE.

K KEY FACTS

- The **order** of a matrix is the number of rows and columns in the matrix. A matrix with order $m \times n$ has m rows and n columns.

- The entries in the matrix are called **elements**.

- Two or more matrices can be added or subtracted if, and only if, they have the same order. To add (or subtract) two matrices, you add (or subtract) the corresponding elements in each matrix.

- A matrix can be multiplied by a scalar (a number). Each element of the matrix is multiplied by the scalar.

- Two matrices can be multiplied only if the number of columns in the first matrix is the same as the number of rows in the second matrix. Matrices which can be multiplied are called *conformable*.

- Unlike multiplication with numbers, matrix multiplication is not *commutative*. This means that the matrix product **AB** is not usually the same as the matrix product **BA**.

- Matrix multiplication is *associative*. This means that $(\mathbf{AB})\mathbf{C} = \mathbf{A}(\mathbf{BC})$ for all matrices **A**, **B** and **C**.

The language of matrices

The **order** of a matrix is the number of rows and columns in the matrix.
A matrix with order $m \times n$ has m rows and n columns.

For example, $\begin{pmatrix} 1 & 1 & -3 \\ -2 & 0 & 2 \end{pmatrix}$ has 2 rows and 3 columns, so this is a 2×3 matrix.

A matrix which has the same number of rows and columns is called a **square** matrix.

Two matrices are **equal** if, and only if, each element in one matrix is equal to the corresponding element in the other matrix.

The matrix $\begin{pmatrix} 0 & 0 \\ 0 & 0 \end{pmatrix}$ is called the 2×2 **zero matrix**.

Adding and subtracting matrices

You can add (or subtract) two matrices by adding (or subtracting) the corresponding elements. You can only do this if the two matrices have the same order, as in the following two examples.

$$\begin{pmatrix} 1 & 3 & -2 \\ 4 & 1 & 0 \end{pmatrix} + \begin{pmatrix} 2 & -1 & 3 \\ 0 & 4 & -2 \end{pmatrix} = \begin{pmatrix} 3 & 2 & 1 \\ 4 & 5 & -2 \end{pmatrix}$$

$$\begin{pmatrix} 1 & 0 \\ -3 & 2 \end{pmatrix} - \begin{pmatrix} -4 & 3 \\ -1 & 1 \end{pmatrix} = \begin{pmatrix} 5 & -3 \\ -2 & 1 \end{pmatrix}$$

Multiplying by a scalar

A matrix can be multiplied by a number. This is called *scalar* multiplication. Multiply each element of the matrix by the number.

For example, $\quad 3\begin{pmatrix} 2 & -3 \\ 0 & 1 \end{pmatrix} = \begin{pmatrix} 6 & -9 \\ 0 & 3 \end{pmatrix}$

EXAMPLE 1

Two matrices are $\mathbf{A} = \begin{pmatrix} 1 & 4 \\ 2 & -3 \end{pmatrix}$ and $\mathbf{B} = \begin{pmatrix} 5 & 0 \\ -1 & -2 \end{pmatrix}$.

Find   **i)** $2\mathbf{A} + \mathbf{B}$

       ii) $3\mathbf{B} - 4\mathbf{A}$

SOLUTION

i) $\quad 2\mathbf{A} + \mathbf{B} = 2\begin{pmatrix} 1 & 4 \\ 2 & -3 \end{pmatrix} + \begin{pmatrix} 5 & 0 \\ -1 & -2 \end{pmatrix}$

$$= \begin{pmatrix} 2 & 8 \\ 4 & -6 \end{pmatrix} + \begin{pmatrix} 5 & 0 \\ -1 & -2 \end{pmatrix}$$

$$= \begin{pmatrix} 7 & 8 \\ 3 & -8 \end{pmatrix}$$

ii) $\quad 3\mathbf{B} - 4\mathbf{A} = 3\begin{pmatrix} 5 & 0 \\ -1 & -2 \end{pmatrix} - 4\begin{pmatrix} 1 & 4 \\ 2 & -3 \end{pmatrix}$

$$= \begin{pmatrix} 15 & 0 \\ -3 & -6 \end{pmatrix} - \begin{pmatrix} 4 & 16 \\ 8 & -12 \end{pmatrix}$$

$$= \begin{pmatrix} 11 & -16 \\ -11 & 6 \end{pmatrix}$$

Multiplying matrices

Two matrices can be multiplied if they are *conformable*, which means that the number of columns in the first matrix is the same as the number of rows in the second matrix.

> To find the first element, multiply each element in the first row of the first matrix by the corresponding element in the first column of the second matrix, and add these up.

$$\begin{pmatrix} 3 & 1 \\ -2 & 4 \end{pmatrix}\begin{pmatrix} 2 & 0 & -3 \\ 5 & -1 & 6 \end{pmatrix} = \begin{pmatrix} 3 \times 2 + 1 \times 5 & \ldots & \ldots \\ \ldots & \ldots & \ldots \end{pmatrix}$$

Continue in the same way. You find the element in row m and column n using row m of the first matrix and column n of the second matrix.

> With practice you can do this stage in your head.

$$\begin{pmatrix} 3 & 1 \\ -2 & 4 \end{pmatrix}\begin{pmatrix} 2 & 0 & -3 \\ 5 & -1 & 6 \end{pmatrix} = \begin{pmatrix} 3 \times 2 + 1 \times 5 & 3 \times 0 + 1 \times -1 & 3 \times -3 + 1 \times 6 \\ -2 \times 2 + 4 \times 5 & -2 \times 0 + 4 \times -1 & -2 \times -3 + 4 \times 6 \end{pmatrix}$$

$$= \begin{pmatrix} 11 & -1 & -3 \\ 16 & -4 & 30 \end{pmatrix}$$

EXAMPLE 2

Given the matrices $\mathbf{A} = \begin{pmatrix} 2 & -1 & 1 \\ 0 & 3 & 4 \end{pmatrix}$, $\mathbf{B} = \begin{pmatrix} 0 & -1 \\ 2 & 3 \\ 1 & -3 \end{pmatrix}$ and $\mathbf{C} = \begin{pmatrix} 1 & 0 \\ 4 & -2 \end{pmatrix}$, find, where possible, the following matrix products.

   i)   **AB**   **ii)**   **BA**   **iii)**   **BC**   **iv)**   **CB**

> $(2 \times 0) + (-1 \times 2) + (1 \times 1) = 0 - 2 + 1 = -1$

SOLUTION

i) $\mathbf{AB} = \begin{pmatrix} 2 & -1 & 1 \\ 0 & 3 & 4 \end{pmatrix}\begin{pmatrix} 0 & -1 \\ 2 & 3 \\ 1 & -3 \end{pmatrix} = \begin{pmatrix} -1 & -8 \\ 10 & -3 \end{pmatrix}$

ii) $\mathbf{BA} = \begin{pmatrix} 0 & -1 \\ 2 & 3 \\ 1 & -3 \end{pmatrix}\begin{pmatrix} 2 & -1 & 1 \\ 0 & 3 & 4 \end{pmatrix} = \begin{pmatrix} 0 & -3 & -4 \\ 4 & 7 & 14 \\ 2 & -10 & -11 \end{pmatrix}$

iii) $\mathbf{BC} = \begin{pmatrix} 0 & -1 \\ 2 & 3 \\ 1 & -3 \end{pmatrix}\begin{pmatrix} 1 & 0 \\ 4 & -2 \end{pmatrix} = \begin{pmatrix} -4 & 2 \\ 14 & -6 \\ -11 & 6 \end{pmatrix}$

iv)   **CB** cannot be found because **C** is a 2×2 matrix and **B** is a 3×2 matrix.
These matrices are not conformable.

From Example 2, notice that
- The result of multiplying a matrix of order $m \times n$ by a matrix of order $n \times p$ is a matrix of order $m \times p$.
- Parts **iii)** and **iv)** show that matrix multiplication is not **commutative**, i.e. for two matrices **P** and **Q**, it is usually the case that **PQ** $\neq$ **QP**. Sometimes **PQ** might not exist when **QP** does.

Although matrix multiplication is not commutative, it is **associative**, which means that **P(QR)** = **(PQ)R** for all matrices **P**, **Q** and **R**.

For example, $\begin{pmatrix} 2 & 1 \\ 3 & 0 \end{pmatrix}\left[\begin{pmatrix} -1 & 2 \\ 4 & 1 \end{pmatrix}\begin{pmatrix} 5 & 3 \\ -2 & 1 \end{pmatrix}\right] = \begin{pmatrix} 2 & 1 \\ 3 & 0 \end{pmatrix}\begin{pmatrix} -9 & -1 \\ 18 & 13 \end{pmatrix} = \begin{pmatrix} 0 & 11 \\ -27 & -3 \end{pmatrix}$

$\left[\begin{pmatrix} 2 & 1 \\ 3 & 0 \end{pmatrix}\begin{pmatrix} -1 & 2 \\ 4 & 1 \end{pmatrix}\right]\begin{pmatrix} 5 & 3 \\ -2 & 1 \end{pmatrix} = \begin{pmatrix} 2 & 5 \\ -3 & 6 \end{pmatrix}\begin{pmatrix} 5 & 3 \\ -2 & 1 \end{pmatrix} = \begin{pmatrix} 0 & 11 \\ -27 & -3 \end{pmatrix}$

LINKS

Pure Mathematics   This work is fundamental to the rest of the work on matrices in both FP1 and FP2. Matrix multiplication is used in the FP2 work on Markov chains.

Test Yourself

1 Two matrices are defined as $\mathbf{M} = \begin{pmatrix} 1 & -3 \\ 2 & 0 \end{pmatrix}$ and $\mathbf{N} = \begin{pmatrix} -2 & 1 \\ 4 & 3 \end{pmatrix}$.

What is the matrix $3\mathbf{M} - 2\mathbf{N}$?

  A $\begin{pmatrix} 7 & -11 \\ -2 & -3 \end{pmatrix}$ **B** $\begin{pmatrix} 1 & 7 \\ 14 & 6 \end{pmatrix}$ **C** $\begin{pmatrix} 7 & -11 \\ -2 & -6 \end{pmatrix}$ **D** $\begin{pmatrix} -1 & 11 \\ -2 & -6 \end{pmatrix}$

Questions 2, 3, 4 and 5 are about the following matrices:

$$P = \begin{pmatrix} 2 & 1 \\ 3 & -2 \end{pmatrix} \qquad Q = \begin{pmatrix} 4 & -1 \\ 2 & 3 \\ 0 & 1 \end{pmatrix} \qquad R = \begin{pmatrix} -2 & 5 & 1 \\ 3 & 0 & 2 \end{pmatrix} \qquad S = \begin{pmatrix} 0 & 1 & 2 \\ 4 & -3 & 0 \\ -1 & -2 & 3 \end{pmatrix}$$

2 What is the matrix product **QR**?

A $\begin{pmatrix} -8 & -3 \\ 10 & 0 \\ 0 & 2 \end{pmatrix}$ 　　B $\begin{pmatrix} -8 & 10 & 0 \\ -3 & 0 & 2 \end{pmatrix}$ 　　C $\begin{pmatrix} -11 & 20 & 2 \\ 5 & 10 & 8 \\ 3 & 0 & 2 \end{pmatrix}$ 　　D $\begin{pmatrix} 2 & 18 \\ 12 & -1 \end{pmatrix}$

E **QR** cannot be found

3 What is the matrix product **QP**?

A $\begin{pmatrix} 5 & 13 & 3 \\ 6 & -4 & -2 \end{pmatrix}$ 　　B $\begin{pmatrix} 5 & 6 \\ 13 & -4 \\ 3 & -2 \end{pmatrix}$ 　　C $\begin{pmatrix} 7 & 14 \\ 7 & 0 \\ 1 & -2 \end{pmatrix}$ 　　D $\begin{pmatrix} 7 & 7 & 1 \\ 14 & 0 & -2 \end{pmatrix}$

E **QP** cannot be found

4 What is the matrix product **RS**?

A $\begin{pmatrix} 7 & -23 & -5 \\ 4 & 12 & 3 \end{pmatrix}$ 　　B $\begin{pmatrix} 19 & -2 \\ -19 & -1 \\ -1 & 12 \end{pmatrix}$ 　　C $\begin{pmatrix} 19 & -19 & -1 \\ -2 & -1 & 12 \end{pmatrix}$ 　　D $\begin{pmatrix} 7 & 4 \\ -23 & 12 \\ -5 & 3 \end{pmatrix}$

E **RS** cannot be found

5 One of the statements below is true and the other three are false. Which statement is true?

A The matrices **RQ** + **P** and **SQ** + **R** both exist.

B The matrix **RQ** + **P** exists but the matrix **SQ** + **R** does not.

C The matrix **RQ** + **P** does not exist but the matrix **SQ** + **R** does.

D Neither of the matrices **RQ** + **P** and **SQ** + **R** exists.

Exam-Style Question DL

You are given the matrices:

$$A = \begin{pmatrix} 3 & 1 \\ 0 & -2 \end{pmatrix}, B = \begin{pmatrix} 4 & 3 \\ -1 & 1 \end{pmatrix}, C = \begin{pmatrix} 1 & 0 & -3 \\ 2 & -1 & 0 \end{pmatrix}, D = (4 \quad -2 \quad 0), E = \begin{pmatrix} 2 \\ 3 \\ -1 \end{pmatrix}.$$

i)   Calculate, where possible, **A** − **B**, **B** + **C**, 2**A**, **BC**, **CA** and **DE**.

ii) Show that matrix multiplication is not commutative.

Transformations

K | **KEY FACTS**

- Any 2 × 2 matrix can be used to represent a transformation in the x–y plane. If a transformation is represented by the matrix $\begin{pmatrix} a & c \\ b & d \end{pmatrix}$ then the image of any point (x, y) under that transformation is given by $\begin{pmatrix} a & c \\ b & d \end{pmatrix}\begin{pmatrix} x \\ y \end{pmatrix} = \begin{pmatrix} x' \\ y' \end{pmatrix}$, where (x', y') are the co-ordinates of the image of (x, y).
- You should be familiar with the matrices representing reflections in the co-ordinate axes or in the lines $y = x$ or $y = -x$; enlargements centre the origin; and rotations centre the origin through any angle.
- The first column of a transformation matrix is given by the image of the point $(1, 0)$ under the transformation, and the second column is given by the image of the point $(0, 1)$ under the transformation.
- The matrix $\mathbf{I} = \begin{pmatrix} 1 & 0 \\ 0 & 1 \end{pmatrix}$ is called the 2 × 2 **identity matrix**. It maps every point to itself. For every matrix $\mathbf{M}$, $\mathbf{IM} = \mathbf{MI} = \mathbf{M}$.
- If a transformation represented by matrix $\mathbf{P}$ is followed by a second transformation represented by matrix $\mathbf{Q}$, the combined transformation is represented by the matrix $\mathbf{QP}$.

Finding image points

The image of any point under a transformation can be found by pre-multiplying the 2 × 1 matrix representing the point by the 2 × 2 matrix representing the transformation.

For example, the image of the point (2, −3) under the transformation

represented by $\begin{pmatrix} 3 & 1 \\ -2 & 4 \end{pmatrix}$ $\boxed{\text{The object point}}$

is given by $\begin{pmatrix} 3 & 1 \\ -2 & 4 \end{pmatrix}\begin{pmatrix} 2 \\ -3 \end{pmatrix}$ $\begin{pmatrix} 3 \\ -16 \end{pmatrix}$ $\boxed{\text{The image point}}$

So the image of the point (2, −3) under this transformation is (3, − 16).

You can calculate the images of several points at once, by writing them as a matrix in which each column represents a point. This is shown in the following example.

EXAMPLE 1

A triangle has vertices A(2, 0), B(1, 3) and C(−1, −2). The triangle is transformed using the matrix $\begin{pmatrix} 3 & 0 \\ -1 & 1 \end{pmatrix}$.

i) Find the images A′, B′ and C′ of the points A, B and C.

ii) Draw the triangle ABC and its image A′B′C′ on the same diagram.

SOLUTION

i) $\begin{pmatrix} 3 & 0 \\ -1 & 1 \end{pmatrix} \begin{pmatrix} 2 & 1 & -1 \\ 0 & 3 & -2 \end{pmatrix} = \begin{pmatrix} 6 & 3 & -3 \\ -2 & 2 & -1 \end{pmatrix}$

The image points are A′(6, −2), B′(3, 2) and C′(−3, −1).

> The three columns of this matrix represent the points A, B and C.

> The three columns of this matrix represent the images A′, B′ and C′.

ii)

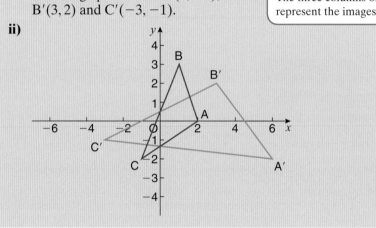

Finding a matrix to represent a transformation

For any matrix $\begin{pmatrix} a & c \\ b & d \end{pmatrix}$, the image of the point (1, 0) is given by

$$\begin{pmatrix} a & c \\ b & d \end{pmatrix} \begin{pmatrix} 1 \\ 0 \end{pmatrix} = \begin{pmatrix} a \\ b \end{pmatrix}.$$

So the image of the point (1, 0) is the first column of the matrix.

Similarly, the image of the point (0, 1) is given by $\begin{pmatrix} a & c \\ b & d \end{pmatrix} \begin{pmatrix} 0 \\ 1 \end{pmatrix} = \begin{pmatrix} c \\ d \end{pmatrix}.$

So the image of the point (0, 1) is the second column of the matrix.

This provides a quick method of finding the matrix representing a simple transformation.

EXAMPLE 2

Find the matrices representing the following transformations.

i) A rotation of 90° anticlockwise about the origin.

ii) A reflection in the line $y = -x$.

iii) An enlargement, centre the origin, scale factor 2.

SOLUTION

i) The image of the point $(1, 0)$ under this rotation is the point $(0, 1)$.
The image of the point $(0, 1)$ under this rotation is the point $(-1, 0)$.
So the matrix representing this rotation is $\begin{pmatrix} 0 & -1 \\ 1 & 0 \end{pmatrix}$.

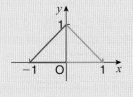

ii) The image of the point $(1, 0)$ under this reflection is the point $(0, -1)$.
The image of the point $(0, 1)$ under this reflection is the point $(-1, 0)$.
So the matrix representing this reflection is $\begin{pmatrix} 0 & -1 \\ -1 & 0 \end{pmatrix}$.

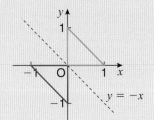

iii) The image of the point $(1, 0)$ under this enlargement is the point $(2, 0)$.
The image of the point $(0, 1)$ under this enlargement is the point $(0, 2)$.
So the matrix representing this enlargement is $\begin{pmatrix} 2 & 0 \\ 0 & 2 \end{pmatrix}$.

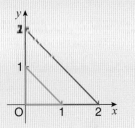

General rotations

The matrix $\begin{pmatrix} \cos\theta & -\sin\theta \\ \sin\theta & \cos\theta \end{pmatrix}$ represents a rotation anticlockwise about the origin through angle θ. This matrix is given in your formula book.

EXAMPLE 3

Describe fully the transformations described by the matrices

i) $\begin{pmatrix} 2 & 0 \\ 0 & 3 \end{pmatrix}$ ii) $\begin{pmatrix} -\frac{1}{2} & -\frac{\sqrt{3}}{2} \\ \frac{\sqrt{3}}{2} & -\frac{1}{2} \end{pmatrix}$.

SOLUTION

i) The image of the point (x, y) is given by $\begin{pmatrix} 2 & 0 \\ 0 & 3 \end{pmatrix}\begin{pmatrix} x \\ y \end{pmatrix} = \begin{pmatrix} 2x \\ 3y \end{pmatrix}$.
So the transformation is a two-way stretch, with scale factor 2 in the x direction, and scale factor 3 in the y direction.

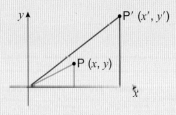

ii) Compare the matrix $\begin{pmatrix} -\frac{1}{2} & -\frac{\sqrt{3}}{2} \\ \frac{\sqrt{3}}{2} & -\frac{1}{2} \end{pmatrix}$ with the general rotation

matrix $\begin{pmatrix} \cos\theta & -\sin\theta \\ \sin\theta & \cos\theta \end{pmatrix}$.

The transformation represents a rotation about the origin through angle θ, where $\cos\theta = -\frac{1}{2}$ and $\sin\theta = \frac{\sqrt{3}}{2}$. Since θ has a negative cosine and a positive sine, it must lie in the second quadrant. Therefore $\theta = 120°$.
The matrix represents a rotation of $120°$ anticlockwise about the origin.

Combined transformations

The result of applying a transformation represented by the matrix **P** followed by a second transformation represented by the matrix **Q** can be represented by the matrix product **QP**.

> ⚠ Make sure that you multiply the matrices in the correct order. The first transformation is the matrix on the right.

EXAMPLE 4

Two transformations are represented by the matrices $\mathbf{S} = \begin{pmatrix} 1 & 2 \\ 0 & 1 \end{pmatrix}$ and $\mathbf{T} = \begin{pmatrix} 2 & 0 \\ 1 & 1 \end{pmatrix}$.

Find the matrix representing **S** followed by **T**.

SOLUTION

The result of **S** followed by **T** is the matrix $\mathbf{TS} = \begin{pmatrix} 2 & 0 \\ 1 & 1 \end{pmatrix}\begin{pmatrix} 1 & 2 \\ 0 & 1 \end{pmatrix} = \begin{pmatrix} 2 & 4 \\ 1 & 3 \end{pmatrix}$.

LINKS

Pure Mathematics

This work is developed further in the next two sections, on inverse matrices and transformations.

Test Yourself ▷L

1 Which of the following is the correct description for the matrix $\begin{pmatrix} 1 & 0 \\ 0 & -1 \end{pmatrix}$?

A Rotation through 90° clockwise about the origin

B Rotation through 90° anticlockwise about the origin

C Reflection in the x axis

D Reflection in the y axis

2 What is the matrix which represents a rotation through 180° about the origin?

A $\begin{pmatrix} 0 & 1 \\ 1 & 0 \end{pmatrix}$ B $\begin{pmatrix} -1 & 0 \\ 0 & -1 \end{pmatrix}$ C $\begin{pmatrix} 0 & -1 \\ -1 & 0 \end{pmatrix}$ D $\begin{pmatrix} -1 & 0 \\ 0 & 1 \end{pmatrix}$

3 Which of the following is the correct description for the matrix $\begin{pmatrix} 0 & 1 \\ -1 & 0 \end{pmatrix}$?

A Rotation through 90° clockwise about the origin

B Rotation through 90° anticlockwise about the origin

C Reflection in the x axis

D Reflection in the y axis

4 What is the matrix which represents a rotation through 150° anticlockwise about the origin, followed by an enlargement, centre the origin, scale factor 2?

A $\begin{pmatrix} \sqrt{3} & -1 \\ 1 & \sqrt{3} \end{pmatrix}$ B $\begin{pmatrix} \sqrt{3} & 1 \\ -1 & \sqrt{3} \end{pmatrix}$ C $\begin{pmatrix} -\sqrt{3} & -1 \\ 1 & -\sqrt{3} \end{pmatrix}$ D $\begin{pmatrix} -\sqrt{3} & 1 \\ -1 & -\sqrt{3} \end{pmatrix}$

5 What is the matrix which represents a reflection in the line $y = x$ followed by the transformation represented by the matrix $\begin{pmatrix} 1 & 2 \\ -1 & 3 \end{pmatrix}$?

A $\begin{pmatrix} -1 & 3 \\ 1 & 2 \end{pmatrix}$ B $\begin{pmatrix} -2 & -1 \\ -3 & 1 \end{pmatrix}$ C $\begin{pmatrix} -1 & -2 \\ 1 & -3 \end{pmatrix}$ D $\begin{pmatrix} 2 & 1 \\ 3 & -1 \end{pmatrix}$ E $\begin{pmatrix} 1 & -3 \\ -1 & -2 \end{pmatrix}$

Exam-Style Question ➤L

i) Write down the 2×2 matrix for reflection in the y axis.

ii) A composite transformation is formed by the transformation represented by the matrix $\begin{pmatrix} 0.5 & \frac{\sqrt{3}}{2} \\ \frac{\sqrt{3}}{2} & -0.5 \end{pmatrix}$ followed by a reflection in the y axis. Find the single matrix that represents this composite transformation.

iii) Describe fully the single transformation represented by the matrix found in part ii).

Inverse matrices and simultaneous equations

A ABOUT THIS TOPIC

This section is about finding the inverse of a matrix, and the use of inverse matrices to solve simultaneous equations.

R REMEMBER

- The work covered in the previous two sections.

K KEY FACTS

- The inverse of a matrix $\mathbf{M}$ is written as $\mathbf{M}^{-1}$, and satisfies $\mathbf{MM}^{-1} = \mathbf{M}^{-1}\mathbf{M} = \mathbf{I}$.

- The **determinant** of the matrix $\begin{pmatrix} a & c \\ b & d \end{pmatrix}$ is given by $ad - bc$.

- If the determinant of a matrix is zero, the matrix has no inverse and is called **singular**.

- The inverse of a non-singular 2×2 matrix $\begin{pmatrix} a & c \\ b & d \end{pmatrix}$ is $\dfrac{1}{ad - bc} \begin{pmatrix} d & -c \\ -b & a \end{pmatrix}$.

- For any two non-singular matrices $\mathbf{M}$ and $\mathbf{N}$, $(\mathbf{MN})^{-1} = \mathbf{N}^{-1}\mathbf{M}^{-1}$.

- A set of simultaneous equations can be written as a matrix equation, which can be solved using the inverse matrix. If the matrix is singular, the equations do not have a unique solution. They may have no solution, or infinitely many solutions.

The inverse of a matrix

The inverse of a matrix 'undoes' the effect of the matrix.

Multiplying a 2×2 matrix by its inverse (in either order) gives the 2×2 identity matrix $\begin{pmatrix} 1 & 0 \\ 0 & 1 \end{pmatrix}$.

Multiplying a 3×3 matrix by its inverse (in either order) gives the 3×3 identity matrix $\begin{pmatrix} 1 & 0 & 0 \\ 0 & 1 & 0 \\ 0 & 0 & 1 \end{pmatrix}$, and similarly for square matrices of any size.

The inverse of a 2×2 matrix

The inverse of a 2×2 matrix $\begin{pmatrix} a & c \\ b & d \end{pmatrix}$ is given by $\dfrac{1}{ad - bc} \begin{pmatrix} d & -c \\ -b & a \end{pmatrix}$.

> Swap the elements on the top left to bottom right diagonal, and change the sign of each element on the other diagonal.

The quantity $ad - bc$ is called the determinant of the matrix. The determinant of a matrix $\mathbf{M}$ is written as det $\mathbf{M}$ or as $|\mathbf{M}|$.

If the determinant of the matrix is zero, then the matrix has no inverse, and it is called a **singular** matrix.

EXAMPLE 1

Find, if possible, the inverses of the matrices $\mathbf{A} = \begin{pmatrix} 3 & -1 \\ 4 & -2 \end{pmatrix}$ and $\mathbf{B} = \begin{pmatrix} 2 & -4 \\ -3 & 6 \end{pmatrix}$.

SOLUTION

$\det \mathbf{A} = (3 \times -2) - (4 \times -1) = -6 + 4 = -2$,

so $\mathbf{A}^{-1} = \frac{1}{-2} \begin{pmatrix} -2 & 1 \\ -4 & 3 \end{pmatrix} = \begin{pmatrix} 1 & -\frac{1}{2} \\ 2 & -\frac{3}{2} \end{pmatrix}$

$\det \mathbf{B} = (2 \times 6) - (-3 \times -4) = 12 - 12 = 0$

Since the determinant of $\mathbf{B}$ is zero, the matrix is singular and has no inverse.

The inverse of a product

For any two non-singular matrices $\mathbf{M}$ and $\mathbf{N}$, $(\mathbf{MN})^{-1} = \mathbf{N}^{-1}\mathbf{M}^{-1}$

> The order of the matrices is reversed. $\mathbf{MN}$ represents $\mathbf{N}$ followed by $\mathbf{M}$, and $\mathbf{N}^{-1}\mathbf{M}^{-1}$ represents undoing $\mathbf{M}$, then undoing $\mathbf{N}$.

For example, the inverse of $\mathbf{P} = \begin{pmatrix} 5 & 2 \\ 2 & 1 \end{pmatrix}$ is $\mathbf{P}^{-1} = \begin{pmatrix} 1 & -2 \\ -2 & 5 \end{pmatrix}$,

and the inverse of $\mathbf{Q} = \begin{pmatrix} 3 & 1 \\ -2 & 0 \end{pmatrix}$ is $\mathbf{Q}^{-1} = \begin{pmatrix} 0 & -\frac{1}{2} \\ 1 & \frac{3}{2} \end{pmatrix}$.

$\mathbf{PQ} = \begin{pmatrix} 5 & 2 \\ 2 & 1 \end{pmatrix}\begin{pmatrix} 3 & 1 \\ -2 & 0 \end{pmatrix} = \begin{pmatrix} 11 & 5 \\ 4 & 2 \end{pmatrix}$, and its inverse $(\mathbf{PQ})^{-1} = \begin{pmatrix} 1 & -\frac{5}{2} \\ -2 & \frac{11}{2} \end{pmatrix}$.

$\mathbf{Q}^{-1}\mathbf{P}^{-1} = \begin{pmatrix} 0 & -\frac{1}{2} \\ 1 & \frac{3}{2} \end{pmatrix}\begin{pmatrix} 1 & -2 \\ -2 & 5 \end{pmatrix} = \begin{pmatrix} 1 & -\frac{5}{2} \\ -2 & \frac{11}{2} \end{pmatrix}$, so $(\mathbf{PQ})^{-1} = \mathbf{Q}^{-1}\mathbf{P}^{-1}$.

Matrices and simultaneous equations

Systems of simultaneous equations can be solved by writing the equations as a single matrix equation and then using an inverse matrix to solve the matrix equation. **Example 3** shows how this is done for two equations in two unknowns.

EXAMPLE 2

Use a matrix method to solve these simultaneous equations.
$$2x - 3y = 8$$
$$5x + y = 3$$

SOLUTION

The equations can be written as the matrix equation $\begin{pmatrix} 2 & -3 \\ 5 & 1 \end{pmatrix}\begin{pmatrix} x \\ y \end{pmatrix} = \begin{pmatrix} 8 \\ 3 \end{pmatrix}$.

$\det \begin{pmatrix} 2 & -3 \\ 5 & 1 \end{pmatrix} = (2 \times 1) - (5 \times -3) = 2 + 15 = 17$

So $\begin{pmatrix} 2 & -3 \\ 5 & 1 \end{pmatrix}^{-1} = \frac{1}{17}\begin{pmatrix} 1 & 3 \\ -5 & 2 \end{pmatrix}$

> It's easier to leave the $\frac{1}{17}$ outside the matrix at this stage.

Pre-multiplying both sides of the matrix equation by the inverse matrix:

$\frac{1}{17}\begin{pmatrix} 1 & 3 \\ -5 & 2 \end{pmatrix}\begin{pmatrix} 2 & -3 \\ 5 & 1 \end{pmatrix}\begin{pmatrix} x \\ y \end{pmatrix} = \frac{1}{17}\begin{pmatrix} 1 & 3 \\ -5 & 2 \end{pmatrix}\begin{pmatrix} 8 \\ 3 \end{pmatrix}$

> Multiplying a matrix by its inverse gives the identity matrix.

$\begin{pmatrix} x \\ y \end{pmatrix} = \frac{1}{17}\begin{pmatrix} 17 \\ -34 \end{pmatrix} = \begin{pmatrix} 1 \\ -2 \end{pmatrix}$

The solution of the equations is $x = 1, y = -2$.

 In an exam question you will score no marks if you are asked to solve simultaneous equations using a matrix method, but you solve them using a different method.

Solving a pair of linear simultaneous equations represents finding the intersection point of two straight lines.

If the matrix is singular, it has no inverse and the simultaneous equations do not have a unique solution. If this happens, there are two possible geometrical interpretations:
- The equations represent two parallel lines, in which case there is no solution.
- The equations represent the same line, in which case all points on the line are solutions, so there are an infinite number of solutions.

This method can be used to solve any number of simultaneous equations, provided the number of equations equals the number of unknowns. In FP1 you are not required to find an inverse matrix for any matrix greater than 2×2 without help, but you might be given help to find the inverse of a 3×3 matrix, as shown in the next example.

EXAMPLE 3

i) Given that $\begin{pmatrix} -9 & -2 & 8 \\ 5 & 1 & -4 \\ 8 & 2 & k \end{pmatrix}$ is the inverse of $\begin{pmatrix} 1 & 2 & 0 \\ 3 & -1 & 4 \\ 2 & 2 & 1 \end{pmatrix}$, find the value of k.

ii) Hence find the solution of these equations.
$$x + 2y = 3$$
$$3x - y + 4z = 8$$
$$2x + 2y + z = 5$$

SOLUTION

i) $\begin{pmatrix} -9 & -2 & 8 \\ 5 & 1 & -4 \\ 8 & 2 & k \end{pmatrix}\begin{pmatrix} 1 & 2 & 0 \\ 3 & -1 & 4 \\ 2 & 2 & 1 \end{pmatrix} = \begin{pmatrix} 1 & 0 & 0 \\ 0 & 1 & 0 \\ 14 + 2k & 14 + 2k & 8 + k \end{pmatrix}$

The product of a matrix and its inverse is the identity matrix $\begin{pmatrix} 1 & 0 & 0 \\ 0 & 1 & 0 \\ 0 & 0 & 1 \end{pmatrix}$, so $k = -7$.

ii) The equations can be written as: $\begin{pmatrix} 1 & 2 & 0 \\ 3 & -1 & 4 \\ 2 & 2 & 1 \end{pmatrix}\begin{pmatrix} x \\ y \\ z \end{pmatrix} = \begin{pmatrix} 3 \\ 8 \\ 5 \end{pmatrix}$

Pre-multiplying both sides of the matrix equation by the inverse matrix:

$\begin{pmatrix} -9 & -2 & 8 \\ 5 & 1 & -4 \\ 8 & 2 & -7 \end{pmatrix}\begin{pmatrix} 1 & 2 & 0 \\ 3 & -1 & 4 \\ 2 & 2 & 1 \end{pmatrix}\begin{pmatrix} x \\ y \\ z \end{pmatrix} = \begin{pmatrix} -9 & -2 & 8 \\ 5 & 1 & -4 \\ 8 & 2 & -7 \end{pmatrix}\begin{pmatrix} 3 \\ 8 \\ 5 \end{pmatrix}$

$\begin{pmatrix} x \\ y \\ z \end{pmatrix} = \begin{pmatrix} -3 \\ 3 \\ 5 \end{pmatrix}$

The solution is $x = -3$, $y = 3$, $z = 5$.

LINKS

Pure Mathematics   Determinants and inverses of 3×3 matrices are covered in FP2.
The work on simultaneous equations is also developed further in FP2.

Test Yourself ▶L

1 The matrix $\begin{pmatrix} 3 & k \\ -4 & 1-2k \end{pmatrix}$ is singular. What is the value of k?

    A 0.3   B 1.5   C −1.5   D 1

2 Find the inverse of the matrix $\begin{pmatrix} 0 & 1 \\ -2 & 3 \end{pmatrix}$.

    A $\begin{pmatrix} 3 & -1 \\ 2 & 0 \end{pmatrix}$ B $\begin{pmatrix} 0 & -1 \\ 0.5 & -1.5 \end{pmatrix}$ C $\begin{pmatrix} -1.5 & 0.5 \\ -1 & 0 \end{pmatrix}$ D $\begin{pmatrix} 1.5 & -0.5 \\ 1 & 0 \end{pmatrix}$

3 The 2×2 matrix **P** has inverse $\mathbf{P}^{-1} = \begin{pmatrix} 2 & -3 \\ 3 & -4 \end{pmatrix}$.

The 2×2 matrix **Q** has inverse $\mathbf{Q}^{-1} = \begin{pmatrix} 3 & 1 \\ 5 & 2 \end{pmatrix}$.

What is $(\mathbf{PQ})^{-1}$?

    A $\begin{pmatrix} 9 & 4 \\ -11 & -5 \end{pmatrix}$ B $\begin{pmatrix} 5 & 4 \\ 11 & -9 \end{pmatrix}$ C $\begin{pmatrix} 9 & 13 \\ 16 & -23 \end{pmatrix}$ D $\begin{pmatrix} 23 & 13 \\ -16 & 9 \end{pmatrix}$

4 Look at this pair of simultaneous equations.
$$2x - 3y = 4$$
$$5x + 6y = 1$$

Which of the matrix equations below correctly represents these simultaneous equations?

    A $\begin{pmatrix} 2 & 3 \\ 5 & 6 \end{pmatrix}\begin{pmatrix} x \\ y \end{pmatrix} = \begin{pmatrix} 4 \\ 1 \end{pmatrix}$ B $\begin{pmatrix} x \\ y \end{pmatrix}\begin{pmatrix} 2 & -3 \\ 5 & 6 \end{pmatrix} = \begin{pmatrix} 4 \\ 1 \end{pmatrix}$

    C $\begin{pmatrix} 2 & 5 \\ -3 & 6 \end{pmatrix}\begin{pmatrix} x \\ y \end{pmatrix} = \begin{pmatrix} 4 \\ 1 \end{pmatrix}$ D $\begin{pmatrix} 2 & -3 \\ 5 & 6 \end{pmatrix}\begin{pmatrix} x \\ y \end{pmatrix} = \begin{pmatrix} 4 \\ 1 \end{pmatrix}$

Exam-Style Question ▶L

You are given that $\mathbf{A} = \begin{pmatrix} k & -2 & 2 \\ 0 & 4 & -2 \\ -1 & -3 & 1 \end{pmatrix}$ and $\mathbf{B} = \begin{pmatrix} -2 & -4 & -4 \\ 2 & 5 & 6 \\ 4 & 11 & 12 \end{pmatrix}$.

i) Find the matrix **AB**.

ii) Hence write down the inverse matrix $\mathbf{A}^{-1}$ in the case $k = 3$.

iii) Using the result from part **ii)**, solve the following simultaneous equations.
$$3x - 2y + 2z = 2$$
$$4y - 2z = -5$$
$$-x - 3y + z = 5$$

More about transformations

This section brings together some further ideas about matrices and transformations. It looks at the significance of the determinant in matrix transformations, at inverse transformations, transformations with no inverse, and invariant points (points which are unchanged by a transformation).

- The work on inverse matrices in the previous section.

- The determinant of a matrix gives the area scale factor of the corresponding transformation.
- The inverse of a transformation undoes the effect of the transformation. If a transformation is represented by a matrix **M**, the inverse transformation is represented by the inverse matrix $\mathbf{M}^{-1}$.
- A transformation which is represented by a singular matrix has no inverse.
- A point which is unchanged by a transformation is called an **invariant point**.

The meaning of the determinant of a 2 × 2 matrix

The determinant of a 2 × 2 transformation matrix represents the area scale factor of the transformation. So if a shape is transformed using a 2 × 2 matrix, the ratio of the area of the image to the area of the original shape is equal to the determinant of the matrix.

EXAMPLE 1

A transformation that has matrix $\begin{pmatrix} 3 & 1 \\ -4 & 2 \end{pmatrix}$ is applied to a triangle with area 5 square units.
What is the area of the image triangle?

SOLUTION

$\det \begin{pmatrix} 3 & 1 \\ -4 & 2 \end{pmatrix} = (3 \times 2) - (1 \times -4) = 6 + 4 = 10$,

so the area scale factor of the transformation is 10.
Area of image triangle = 5 × 10 = 50 square units.

Inverse transformations

When a matrix represents a transformation, the inverse matrix represents the inverse transformation. So if a matrix **T** maps a point A to its image A′, the inverse matrix $\mathbf{T}^{-1}$ maps the point A′ to the object point A.

Applying a transformation followed by its inverse transformation gives the identity transformation $\mathbf{I} = \begin{pmatrix} 1 & 0 \\ 0 & 1 \end{pmatrix}$, which maps a point to itself.

EXAMPLE 2

The matrix $\mathbf{S} = \begin{pmatrix} 5 & 3 \\ -2 & 1 \end{pmatrix}$ maps the point A to the point $(-4, -5)$.

Find the co-ordinates of A.

SOLUTION

$\det \mathbf{S} = (5 \times 1) - (-2 \times 3) = 5 + 6 = 11$

$\mathbf{S}^{-1} = \frac{1}{11}\begin{pmatrix} 1 & -3 \\ 2 & 5 \end{pmatrix}$

The matrix $\mathbf{S}^{-1}$ maps the point $(-4, -5)$ to the point A.

The image of $(-4, -5)$ under $\mathbf{S}^{-1} = \frac{1}{11}\begin{pmatrix} 1 & -3 \\ 2 & 5 \end{pmatrix}\begin{pmatrix} -4 \\ -5 \end{pmatrix} = \frac{1}{11}\begin{pmatrix} 11 \\ -33 \end{pmatrix} = \begin{pmatrix} 1 \\ -3 \end{pmatrix}$

So the co-ordinates of A are $(1, -3)$.

Transformations involving singular matrices

If a matrix is singular, then it has no inverse. This means that the corresponding transformation has no inverse transformation.

In this type of transformation, all points are mapped to a straight line. This means that an infinite number of points are all mapped to the same point, and therefore the transformation is not one-to-one, and therefore cannot have an inverse transformation, just as a function which is not one-to-one cannot have an inverse function.

EXAMPLE 3

i) Show that the matrix $\begin{pmatrix} 1 & -2 \\ -2 & 4 \end{pmatrix}$ is singular.

ii) Show that this matrix maps all points in the plane on to a straight line, and give the equation of this line.

SOLUTION

i) $\det \begin{pmatrix} 1 & -2 \\ -2 & 4 \end{pmatrix} = (1 \times 4) - (-2 \times -2) = 4 - 4 = 0$

The determinant of the matrix is zero, so the matrix is singular.

ii) The image of a general point (x, y) is given by

$\begin{pmatrix} x' \\ y' \end{pmatrix} = \begin{pmatrix} 1 & -2 \\ -2 & 4 \end{pmatrix}\begin{pmatrix} x \\ y \end{pmatrix} = \begin{pmatrix} x - 2y \\ -2x + 4y \end{pmatrix} = \begin{pmatrix} x - 2y \\ -2(x - 2y) \end{pmatrix}$

So for all image points, $x' = x - 2y$

$y' = -2(x - 2y)$

Dividing $\quad \frac{x'}{y'} = \frac{1}{-2} \rightarrow y' = -2x'$

So all points on the plane are mapped to points on the line $y = -2x$.

Invariant points

An invariant point under a transformation is a point that is mapped to itself.
- In all transformations that can be represented by a 2 × 2 matrix, the origin is an invariant point.
- In a reflection, all points on the mirror line are mapped to themselves. The mirror line is a line of invariant points.
- In rotations and enlargements, the origin is the only invariant point.
- Some other transformations can also have a line of invariant points.

EXAMPLE 4

i) Show that the origin is the only invariant point for the matrix $\begin{pmatrix} 4 & 1 \\ 3 & -2 \end{pmatrix}$.

ii) Find the equation of the line of invariant points for the matrix $\begin{pmatrix} -3 & 2 \\ 4 & -1 \end{pmatrix}$.

SOLUTION

i) For an invariant point, $\begin{pmatrix} 4 & 1 \\ 3 & -2 \end{pmatrix}\begin{pmatrix} x \\ y \end{pmatrix} = \begin{pmatrix} x \\ y \end{pmatrix} \Rightarrow \begin{pmatrix} 4x + y \\ 3x - 2y \end{pmatrix} = \begin{pmatrix} x \\ y \end{pmatrix}$

$$\Rightarrow \begin{cases} 4x + y = x \\ 3x - 2y = y \end{cases}$$

$$\Rightarrow \begin{cases} 3x = -y \\ 3x = 3y \end{cases}$$

The only values of x and y for which both these equations can be true is $x = 0, y = 0$.
So the only invariant point is the origin.

ii) For an invariant point, $\begin{pmatrix} -3 & 2 \\ 4 & -1 \end{pmatrix}\begin{pmatrix} x \\ y \end{pmatrix} = \begin{pmatrix} x \\ y \end{pmatrix} \Rightarrow \begin{pmatrix} -3x + 2y \\ 4x - y \end{pmatrix} = \begin{pmatrix} x \\ y \end{pmatrix}$

$$\Rightarrow \begin{cases} -3x + 2y = x \\ 4x - y = y \end{cases}$$

$$\Rightarrow \begin{cases} 2y = 4x \\ 4x = 2y \end{cases}$$

> These two equations are equivalent.

All points which satisfy the equation $y = 2x$ are invariant points.
So the line $y = 2x$ is a line of invariant points.

Notice that for all transformations which can be represented by matrices, there are only two possibilities: either the origin is the only invariant point (as in the first part of **Example 4**) or there is a line of invariant points (as in part **ii)** of the example).

LINKS

Pure Mathematics   The work on invariant points leads on to further work on eigenvectors and eigenvalues in FP2.

Test Yourself ▶L

1 The transformation associated with the matrix $\begin{pmatrix} 6 & 3 \\ -1 & 2 \end{pmatrix}$ is applied to a figure of area 4 square units. What is the area of the transformed figure?

    A 36 square units   B 60 square units   C 15 square units   D 900 square units

2 A matrix $\begin{pmatrix} 2 & 4 \\ 1 & -3 \end{pmatrix}$ maps a point P to the point $(6, 8)$. Find the co-ordinates of P.

    A $(44, -18)$ B $(25, -5)$ C $(-50, 10)$ D $(5, -1)$

3 The matrix $\begin{pmatrix} 6 & 3 \\ -2 & -1 \end{pmatrix}$ maps all points in the plane onto a straight line. Find the equation of this line.

    A $y = -\frac{1}{3}x$ B $y = \frac{1}{3}x$ C $y = -3x$ D $y = 3x$

4 The matrix $\begin{pmatrix} 3 & 1 \\ 4 & k \end{pmatrix}$ has more than one invariant point. What is the value of k?

    A -1 B 3   C 2   D $\frac{4}{3}$

5 Find the equation of the line of invariant points for the matrix $\begin{pmatrix} 6 & -2 \\ 5 & -1 \end{pmatrix}$.

    A $y = \frac{2}{5}x$ B $y = -x$ C $y = \frac{5}{2}x$ D $y = x$

Exam-Style Question ▶L

A transformation is represented by the matrix $\begin{pmatrix} 4 & 2 \\ -6 & -3 \end{pmatrix}$.

i) Find the image of the point $(5, -3)$ under the transformation.

ii) Find the equation of the line of invariant points of the transformation.

iii) What is the determinant of the matrix?

iv) The transformation maps all points on to the same line. What is the equation of that line?

v) All the points on a particular straight line are mapped to the point $(2, -3)$. Find the equation of this straight line.

Complex numbers

2

Working with complex numbers

▶▶ 48
55, 69
87

A ABOUT THIS TOPIC

Mathematicians introduced a new, imaginary number j which equals $\sqrt{-1}$ to help them solve equations such as $x^2 + 1 = 0$. Even though j is 'imaginary', the mathematics of complex numbers has many applications in the real world, especially in science and engineering. You can use the number j to write complex numbers in the form $x + y$j and in this section you will learn how to add, subtract, multiply and divide complex numbers. You will also learn how to solve quadratic equations which have no real roots.

R REMEMBER

- Solving quadratic equations from GCSE and C1.
- Solving simultaneous equations from GCSE and C1.

K KEY FACTS

- A **complex number**, z, is written in the form $z = x + y$j where x and y are real numbers and $j = \sqrt{-1}$.
  x is the real part of z, written $\text{Re}(z)$, and y is the imaginary part of z, written $\text{Im}(z)$.
- You add and subtract complex numbers by adding and subtracting the real and imaginary parts separately.
- The *conjugate* of $z = x + y$j is $z^\star = x - y$j.
- To multiply complex numbers you expand the brackets and then simplify.
  Remember $j^2 = -1$.
- To divide by a complex number, z, you multiply both the top line and bottom line of the fraction by the conjugate, $z^\star$, of the bottom line. This gives the answer in the form $a + b$j.
- You can use the quadratic formula to find the complex roots of a quadratic equation that has no real roots.

Numbers like $w = 3 - 4$j and $z = -2 - 3$j are called complex numbers.
They have a real and an imaginary part.

For w: $\text{Re}(w) = 3$ and $\text{Im}(w) = -4$ ◄——

> A common mistake is to write $\text{Im}(w) = -4\mathbf{j}$.
> The real and imaginary parts are given by **real** numbers.

> **1** When two complex numbers are equal then both their real parts are equal and their imaginary parts are equal.
> **2** A complex number equals 0 if, and only if, both the real and imaginary parts equal 0.

Adding and subtracting complex numbers

You can add and subtract complex numbers by simply combining the real and imaginary parts separately.

EXAMPLE 1

Two complex numbers, α and β, are given by $\alpha = -2 + 4j$ and $\beta = 3 - 5j$.

Find **i)** $\alpha - \beta$ and **ii)** $3\alpha + 2\beta$ in the form $a + bj$.

SOLUTION

i) $\alpha - \beta = (-2 + 4j) - (3 - 5j)$
$= (-2 - 3) + (4 + 5)j$
$= -5 + 9j$

> Take care with your signs:
> $4j - -5j = 9j$

ii) $3\alpha + 2\beta = 3(-2 + 4j) + 2(3 - 5j)$
$= -6 + 12j + 6 - 10j$
$= 2j$

Multiplying complex numbers

When you multiply together complex numbers you expand the brackets, as you would any pair of brackets, and then simplify the result.

> Remember that since $j = \sqrt{-1}$ then $j^2 = -1$.

EXAMPLE 2

Two complex numbers, α and β, are given by $\alpha = 4 - 3j$ and $\beta = -1 + 2j$.

Find **i)** $\alpha\beta$ and **ii)** α^2 in the form $a + bj$.

SOLUTION

i) $\alpha\beta = (4 - 3j)(-1 + 2j)$
$= -4 + 8j + 3j - 6j^2$
$= -4 + 11j + 6$
$= 2 + 11j$

> $-6j^2 = -6 \times -1 = +6$

ii) $\alpha^2 = (4 - 3j)^2$
$= 16 - 24j + 9j^2$
$= 16 - 24j - 9$
$= 7 - 24j$

The complex conjugate of $z = x + yj$ is defined as $z^* = x - yj$.

EXAMPLE 3

When $z = 3 - 4j$ find **i)** z^* and **ii)** zz^* in the form $a + bj$.

SOLUTION

i) $z^* = 3 + 4j$

ii) $zz^* = (3 - 4j)(3 + 4j)$
$= 9 + 12j - 12j - 16j^2$
$= 9 + 16$
$= 25$

> To find the conjugate just change the sign of the imaginary part.

> Notice this is $3^2 + 4^2$.

> This illustrates the useful result that if $z = x + yj$ then $z^* = x - yj$ and $zz^* = x^2 + y^2$.
> So when you multiply a complex number by its conjugate you end up with a real number.

Dividing complex numbers

You can divide any number by $z = x + y\text{j}$ by multiplying the top line and the bottom line of the fraction by $z^* = x - y\text{j}$ in order to make the bottom line real.

> This is similar to the method of rationalising the denominator, which you met in C1.

EXAMPLE 4

Two complex numbers, α and β, are given by $\alpha = 3 - \text{j}$ and $\beta = -2 + 2\text{j}$. Find $\dfrac{\alpha}{\beta}$ in the form $a + b\text{j}$.

SOLUTION

$$\frac{\alpha}{\beta} = \frac{3 - \text{j}}{-2 + 2\text{j}}$$

> The conjugate of $-2 + 2\text{j}$ is $-2 - 2\text{j}$.

$$= \frac{(3 - \text{j})(-2 - 2\text{j})}{(-2 + 2\text{j})(-2 - 2\text{j})}$$

> Multiply both the top and bottom lines of the fraction by the conjugate of the bottom line, to make the bottom line a real number.

$$= \frac{-6 - 6\text{j} + 2\text{j} + 2\text{j}^2}{8}$$

> Note that because you multiply the top and bottom lines of the fraction by the same number, $-2 - 2\text{j}$, the value of the fraction is unchanged.

$$= \frac{-8 - 4\text{j}}{8}$$

> Remember if $z = a + b\text{j}$,
> $zz^* = a^2 + b^2$ so
> $(-2 + 2\text{j})(-2 - 2\text{j}) = (-2)^2 + 2^2$
> $= 8$

$$= -1 - \tfrac{1}{2}\text{j}$$

EXAMPLE 5

Find real numbers a and b such that $a + b\text{j} = \dfrac{1}{4\text{j}}$.

SOLUTION

$$\frac{1}{4\text{j}} = \frac{1 \times -4\text{j}}{4\text{j} \times -4\text{j}}$$

$$= \frac{-4\text{j}}{16}$$

$$= -\tfrac{1}{4}\text{j}$$

So $a = 0$ and $b = -\tfrac{1}{4}$.

You can solve equations involving complex numbers in the same way that you would solve an ordinary linear equation.

EXAMPLE 6   Solve $8 + jz = 2z + 9j$, giving z in the form $a + bj$.

SOLUTION

$$8 + jz = 2z + 9j$$
$$\Rightarrow -2z + jz = -8 + 9j$$
$$(-2 + j)z = -8 + 9j$$
$$z = \frac{-8 + 9j}{-2 + j}$$

The conjugate of $-2 + j$ is $-2 - j$.

$$= \frac{(-8 + 9j) \times (-2 - j)}{(-2 + j) \times (-2 - j)}$$

Multiply both the top and bottom lines of the fraction by the conjugate of the bottom line to make the bottom line a real number.

$$= \frac{16 + 8j - 18j + 9}{(-2)^2 + 1^2}$$

$$= \frac{25 - 10j}{5}$$

$$\Rightarrow z = 5 - 2j$$

Solving quadratic equations with no real roots

Complex numbers were originally introduced to help with solving equations. You can write the square roots of any negative number in terms of j.

For example, $z^2 = -9 \Rightarrow z = \pm\sqrt{-9}$
$$= \pm\sqrt{9 \times -1}$$
$$= \pm 3j$$

You can use the quadratic formula to solve quadratic equations which have no real roots. These equations have complex roots.

EXAMPLE 7   Solve $z^2 + 4z + 6 = 0$.

SOLUTION

Using the quadratic formula: $z = \dfrac{-4 \pm \sqrt{16 - 4 \times 6}}{2}$

$$\sqrt{-8} = \sqrt{4 \times 2 \times -1}$$
$$= 2\sqrt{2}j$$

$$= \frac{-4 \pm \sqrt{-8}}{2}$$

 Take care when you simplify:
$$\frac{-4 \pm \sqrt{-8}}{2} \neq -2 \pm \sqrt{-4}$$

$$= \frac{-4 \pm 2\sqrt{2}j}{2}$$

$$= -2 \pm \sqrt{2}j$$

Notice the roots are a conjugate pair. This is always true – so if one root is z the other is z^*.

Test Yourself ◗L

1 When $z = 7 - 3j$ find $\text{Im}(z - z^*)$.

   A 0   B $-6j$ C -6 D $6j$ E 6

2 Find $(2 - 4j)^3$, giving your answer in the form $a + bj$.

   A $-88 + 16j$ B $-24 - 112j$ C $-88 - 112j$ D $144 - 112j$ E $8 + 64j$

3 Find the reciprocal of $z = -1 + 2j$, giving your answer in the form $a + bj$.

   A $\frac{1}{3} + \frac{2}{3}j$ B $\frac{1}{5} - \frac{2}{5}j$ C $-1 - \frac{1}{2}j$ D $-\frac{1}{5} - \frac{2}{5}j$

4 Solve $1 - 2z = (8 - z)j$, giving your answer in the form $a + bj$.

   A $z = -\frac{6}{5} - 3j$ B $z = 2 - 3j$ C $z = -2 - 5j$ D $z = \frac{10}{3} - 5j$

5 Find the roots of the quadratic equation $2z^2 - 8z + 9 = 0$ in the form $a + bj$.

   A $z = 2 \pm \frac{\sqrt{2}}{2}j$ B $z = 2 \pm \sqrt{2}j$ C $z = 8 \pm \frac{\sqrt{2}}{2}j$ D $z = 2 \pm 2\sqrt{2}j$

Exam-Style Question ◗L

a) Two complex numbers, α and β, are given by $\alpha = -1 + 3j$ and $\beta = -2 - j$.
Express $\alpha + \beta$, $\alpha\beta$ and $\dfrac{\alpha}{\beta}$ in the form $a + bj$, showing your working clearly.

b) Find the roots of the quadratic equation $z^2 - 4z + 13 = 0$, simplifying your answers as far as possible.

Representing complex numbers geometrically

A ABOUT THIS TOPIC

Complex numbers are given in the form $z = x + yj$ and so you can represent a complex number, z, as the point with Cartesian co-ordinates (x, y). To plot z you need to know either its co-ordinates, or how far it is from the origin and in what direction it lies. You will learn how to find the set of points that all lie a certain distance from the point z, and the set of points which form a certain angle when joined to z.

R REMEMBER

- Vectors and loci from GCSE.
- Trigonometry and radians from C2.

K KEY FACTS

- $z = x + yj$ can be represented on an Argand diagram as the point (x, y) or as the vector $\begin{pmatrix} x \\ y \end{pmatrix}$.

- The distance from $z = x + yj$ to the origin is called the modulus of z or $|z|$ where $|z| = \sqrt{x^2 + y^2}$.
- The distance between two complex numbers z_1 and z_2 is $|z_2 - z_1|$.
- The set of points z for which $|z - (x + yj)| = r$ form a circle, centre (x, y) and radius r.
- The principal argument of z, written arg z, is the angle that the line from the origin to $z = x + yj$ makes with the positive real axes on an Argand diagram. This angle lies in the range $-\pi < \arg z \leqslant \pi$.
- $z = x + yj$ can be rewritten in modulus–argument form as $z = r(\cos \theta + j \sin \theta)$ where $r = |z|$, $\theta = \arg z$, $x = r \cos \theta$ and $y = r \sin \theta$.
- The set of points for which $\arg(z - (x + yj)) = \theta$ forms the half-line joining $x + yj$ to the points z at an angle of θ to the positive real axis but **excluding** the point $x + yj$ itself.

Representing complex numbers as points or vectors on an Argand diagram

You can plot the complex number $z = x + yj$ as the point (x, y) on an Argand diagram.

You can also show $z = x + yj$ as the vector $\begin{pmatrix} x \\ y \end{pmatrix}$ on an Argand diagram. You can use vectors to show the addition and subtraction of complex numbers.

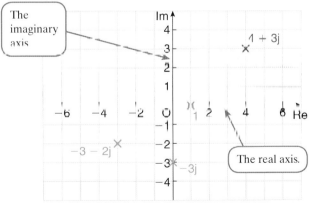

EXAMPLE 1

Two complex numbers, z_1 and z_2, are given by $z_1 = 2 + 4j$ and $z_2 = -3 + 2j$.
Illustrate on an Argand diagram **i)** $z_1 + z_2$ and **ii)** $z_2 - z_1$.

SOLUTION

i) First draw the vectors z_1 and z_2 on an Argand diagram.
Remember $z_1 + z_2$ means go along z_1 and then along z_2.

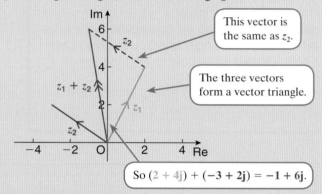

This vector is the same as z_2.

The three vectors form a vector triangle.

So $(2 + 4j) + (-3 + 2j) = -1 + 6j$.

ii) Remember $z_2 - z_1 = z_2 + (-z_1)$.
This diagram illustrates that $z_2 - z_1$ is the vector from z_1 to z_2.

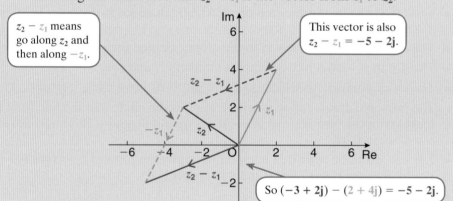

$z_2 - z_1$ means go along z_2 and then along $-z_1$.

This vector is also $z_2 - z_1 = -5 - 2j$.

So $(-3 + 2j) - (2 + 4j) = -5 - 2j$.

The modulus of $z = x + yj$ is $|z| = \sqrt{x^2 + y^2}$.

The distance between two complex numbers $z_1 = x_1 + y_1j$ and
$z_2 = x_2 + y_2j$ is given by:

$$|z_2 - z_1| = \sqrt{(x_2 - x_1)^2 + (y_2 - y_1)^2}.$$

This is from Pythagoras's theorem. It is the distance between the point z and the origin.

EXAMPLE 2

Two complex numbers, α and β, are given by $\alpha = 2 - j$ and $\beta = -1 + 3j$.
Find

i) $|\alpha|$.

You say 'mod α' or 'the modulus of α'.

ii) $|\alpha - \beta|$.

iii) Draw an Argand diagram showing the set of points for
which $|z - \beta| < 5$.

SOLUTION

i) $|\alpha| = |2 - j|$
$= \sqrt{2^2 + (-1)^2}$
$= \sqrt{5}$

> So the distance from α to the origin is $\sqrt{5}$.

ii) $|\alpha - \beta| = |(2 - j) - (-1 + 3j)|$
$= \sqrt{(2 - -1)^2 + (-1 - 3)^2}$
$= \sqrt{3^2 + (-4)^2}$
$= 5$

> So the distance between α and β is 5 units.

> The set of points for which $|z - \beta| < 5$ means all of the points, z, which are **less than** 5 units away from β ...

iii)

> Use a dotted line to show that the circle itself is not included, or explain this clearly next to your diagram.
> Shade the region you need.

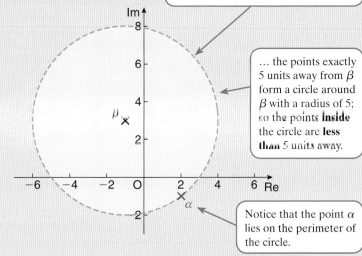

> ... the points exactly 5 units away from β form a circle around β with a radius of 5; so the points **inside** the circle are **less than** 5 units away.

> Notice that the point α lies on the perimeter of the circle.

Circular loci on an Argand diagram

The above example illustrates the general result that the set of points z for which $|z - (x + yj)| = r$ form the perimeter of a circle, centre (x, y) and radius r.

> So $|z - (x + yj)| \geqslant r$ is the perimeter of the circle plus everything outside the circle.

> Take care with your signs!
> For example, $|z - 2 + 4j| = 3$ needs rewriting as $|z - (2 - 4j)| = 3$ to show that it represents a circle centre $(2, -4)$ and radius 3.

Modulus and argument

You can also describe a complex number, $z = x + yj$, on an Argand diagram by giving:
1 its distance from the origin (i.e. the modulus of z, $|z|$) and
2 the angle, θ, that the vector joining the origin to z makes with the positive real axis.

> Angles above the real axis are positive.

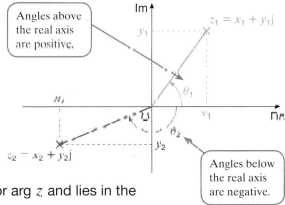

> Angles below the real axis are negative.

The angle, θ, is called the principal argument of z or arg z and lies in the interval $-\pi < \theta \leqslant \pi$.

To work out the value of arg z:
1 Plot z on an Argand diagram to see in which quadrant it lies.

> Make sure you use radians!

2 Work out the value of $\arctan\left(\dfrac{y}{x}\right)$ and use it to find the argument – look at the diagram to help you.

⚠ arg 0 is undefined.

$\dfrac{\pi}{2}$

π

arg $z = \arctan\left(\dfrac{y}{x}\right) + \pi$ arg $z = \arctan\left(\dfrac{y}{x}\right)$

0

arg $z = \arctan\left(\dfrac{y}{x}\right) - \pi$ arg $z = \arctan\left(\dfrac{y}{x}\right)$

$-\dfrac{\pi}{2}$

Im

O

Re

> These show the value of the argument along the axes.

EXAMPLE 3

When $z = -\sqrt{3} + \mathrm{j}$ find the modulus and argument of z.

SOLUTION

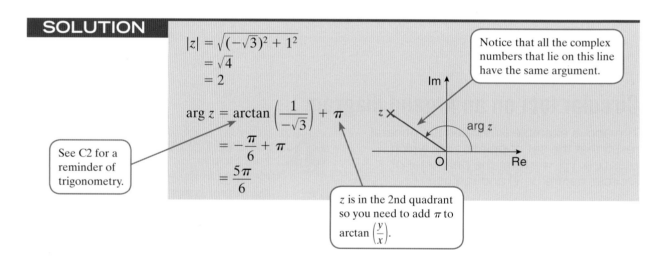

$|z| = \sqrt{(-\sqrt{3})^2 + 1^2}$
$= \sqrt{4}$
$= 2$

$\arg z = \arctan\left(\dfrac{1}{-\sqrt{3}}\right) + \pi$

$= -\dfrac{\pi}{6} + \pi$

$= \dfrac{5\pi}{6}$

> See C2 for a reminder of trigonometry.

> z is in the 2nd quadrant so you need to add π to $\arctan\left(\dfrac{y}{x}\right)$.

> Notice that all the complex numbers that lie on this line have the same argument.

Im

arg z

O

Re

z ✕

The modulus–argument form of a complex number is:

$\quad z = r(\cos\theta + \mathrm{j}\sin\theta)$

where

$\quad r = |z|$ and $\theta = \arg z$

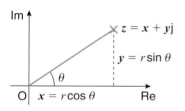

Im

$z = x + y\mathrm{j}$

$y = r\sin\theta$

θ

O $x = r\cos\theta$ Re

EXAMPLE 4

i) Write $z = -2 - 2\mathrm{j}$ in modulus–argument form.

ii) Write $z = 3\left(\cos\left(-\dfrac{\pi}{3}\right) + \mathrm{j}\sin\left(-\dfrac{\pi}{3}\right)\right)$ in the form $z = x + y\mathrm{j}$.

SOLUTION

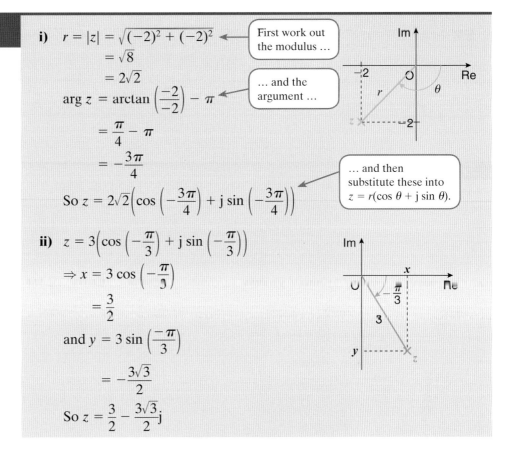

i) $r = |z| = \sqrt{(-2)^2 + (-2)^2}$ ← First work out the modulus …

$$= \sqrt{8}$$

$$= 2\sqrt{2}$$

$\arg z = \arctan\left(\dfrac{-2}{-2}\right) - \pi$ ← … and the argument …

$$= \frac{\pi}{4} - \pi$$

$$= -\frac{3\pi}{4}$$

… and then substitute these into $z = r(\cos\theta + j\sin\theta)$.

So $z = 2\sqrt{2}\left(\cos\left(-\dfrac{3\pi}{4}\right) + j\sin\left(-\dfrac{3\pi}{4}\right)\right)$

ii) $z = 3\left(\cos\left(-\dfrac{\pi}{3}\right) + j\sin\left(-\dfrac{\pi}{3}\right)\right)$

$$\Rightarrow x = 3\cos\left(-\frac{\pi}{3}\right)$$

$$= \frac{3}{2}$$

and $y = 3\sin\left(\dfrac{-\pi}{3}\right)$

$$= -\frac{3\sqrt{3}}{2}$$

So $z = \dfrac{3}{2} - \dfrac{3\sqrt{3}}{2}j$

A ADVICE

When calculating modulus and argument, always check the position of the complex number on an Argand diagram.

Loci involving the argument of a complex number

$\arg(z - (x + yj))$ is the angle between the vector from $x + yj$ to z and the positive real axis.

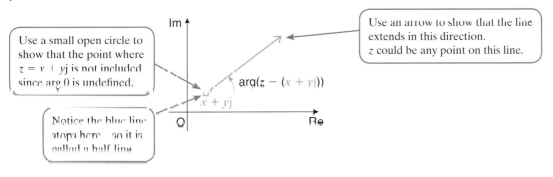

Use a small open circle to show that the point where $z = x + yj$ is not included since arg 0 is undefined.

Notice the blue line stops here — so it is called a half line.

Use an arrow to show that the line extends in this direction. z could be any point on this line.

$\arg(z - (x + yj))$

$x + yj$

EXAMPLE 5

Represent the following loci on separate Argand diagrams:

a) $\arg(z + 1 - 2j) = \dfrac{2\pi}{3}$

b) $\arg(z - (2 - 3j)) \leqslant -\dfrac{\pi}{3}$

SOLUTION

a) You need to rewrite this so it is in the form
$\arg(z - (x + yj))$.

So $\arg(z + 1 - 2j) = \dfrac{2\pi}{3} \Rightarrow \arg(z - (-1 + 2j)) = \dfrac{2\pi}{3}$

This means draw a half-line from the point $(-1, 2)$ making an angle of $\dfrac{2\pi}{3}$ to the positive real axis.

z can be any point along this line except $(-1, 2)$, since arg 0 is undefined.

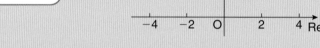

b) $\arg(z - (2 - 3j)) \leqslant -\dfrac{\pi}{3}$

The argument, θ, normally lies in the range $-\pi < \theta \leqslant \pi$, however this question restricts the range so that the maximum value is now $-\dfrac{\pi}{3}$ but the minimum value is still $-\pi$.

So you need to draw half-lines from $(2, -3)$ in the directions $-\pi$ and $-\dfrac{\pi}{3}$.

This line is dotted because the argument cannot actually equal $-\pi$.

The angle of the vector joining $(2, -3)$ to any point in this region will be less than $-\dfrac{\pi}{3}$ to the positive real axis.

LINKS

Complex Numbers   FP2

Test Yourself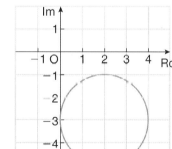

1 You are given that $z_1 = -1 - 2\sqrt{2}j$ and $z_2 = 2 - \sqrt{2}j$.
Find $|z_2 - z_1|$.

   A $\sqrt{11}$ **B** $\sqrt{7}$ **C** $3(\sqrt{2} - 1)$ **D** $3\sqrt{3}$

2 Express $-3 + \sqrt{3}j$ in modulus–argument form.

   A modulus $= 2\sqrt{3}$ and argument $= \dfrac{5\pi}{6}$ **B** $2\sqrt{3}\left(\cos\left(\dfrac{5\pi}{6}\right) + j\sin\left(\dfrac{5\pi}{6}\right)\right)$

   C $2\sqrt{3}\left(\cos\left(\dfrac{\pi}{6}\right) + j\sin\left(\dfrac{\pi}{6}\right)\right)$ **D** $2\sqrt{3}\left(\cos\left(-\dfrac{\pi}{6}\right) + j\sin\left(-\dfrac{\pi}{6}\right)\right)$

   E $\sqrt{2}\sqrt{3}\left(\cos\left(\dfrac{5\pi}{6}\right) + j\sin\left(\dfrac{5\pi}{6}\right)\right)$

3 Represent on an Argand diagram the set of points z for which $\arg(z + 2) = \dfrac{\pi}{4}$.

  A 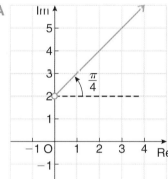   **B**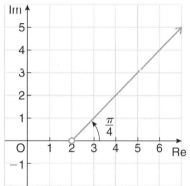

  C 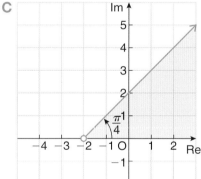   **D**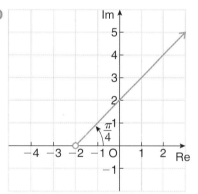

4 Write down the equation of the locus represented by the circle in the Argand diagram.

   A $|z + (2 - 3j)| = 2$

   B $|z - (2 - 3j)| = 4$

   C $|z - (2 - 3j)| = 2$

   D $|z - (2 - 3j)| \leqslant 2$

   E $(x - 2)^2 + (y + 3)^2 = 4$

5 On an Argand diagram sketch the locus of arg $(z - (1 + 2j)) > \dfrac{\pi}{3}$.

A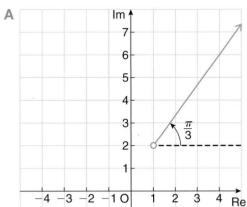

B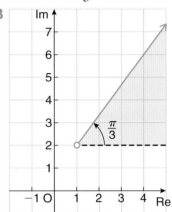

C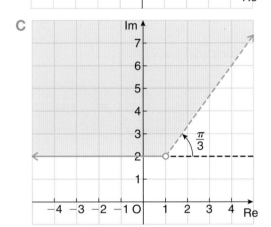

D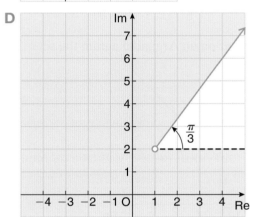

Exam-Style Question

You are given that $\alpha = -2 + 3j$.

i) Express α in modulus–argument form.

ii) Represent the following on separate Argand diagrams.
   A) The set of points z for which $|z - \alpha| = 3$

   B) The set of points z for which $\arg(z - \alpha) = \dfrac{3\pi}{4}$

   C) The set of points z for which $\dfrac{\pi}{4} < \arg(z - \alpha) \leqslant \dfrac{3\pi}{4}$

Complex numbers and equations

A ABOUT THIS TOPIC

You can use your knowledge of complex numbers and the factor theorem from C1 to help you solve polynomial equations which have complex roots.

R REMEMBER

- Solving quadratic equations from GCSE and C1.
- Solving simultaneous equations from GCSE and C1.
- The factor theorem from C1.
- Properties of roots of equations from FP1 (see page 51).

K KEY FACTS

- A polynomial of degree n has n roots (including repeated roots and complex roots).
- The complex roots of a polynomial equation with real coefficients form conjugate pairs.

The total number of roots (including repeated roots and complex roots) is the same as the degree of the polynomial. So a quadratic has two roots, a cubic has three roots, and so on.

The complex roots of a polynomial equation with real coefficients form conjugate pairs.
So if you know that $z = x + y$j is a root
then $z^\star = x - y$j is also a root.

EXAMPLE 1

i) Verify that $2 - 3$j is a root of $3z^3 - 13z^2 + 43z - 13 = 0$.

ii) Write down the other complex root.

iii) Explain why the equation must have a real root.

SOLUTION

i) First find z^2 and z^3:
$$z^2 = (2 - 3j)^2$$
$$= 4 - 12j - 9$$
$$= -5 - 12j$$

Take care with your signs:
$(-3j) \times (-3j) = 9j^2$
$= -9$

$$z^3 = z \times z^2$$
$$= (2 - 3j)(-5 - 12j)$$
$$= -10 - 24j + 15j - 36$$
$$= -46 - 9j$$

Then substitute into the cubic equation:
$$3z^3 - 13z^2 + 43z - 13$$
$$= 3(-46 - 9j) - 13(-5 - 12j) + 43(2 - 3j) - 13$$
$$= -138 - 27j + 65 + 156j + 86 - 129j - 13$$
$$= 0 \text{ as required.}$$

Remember from C1:
if $z = 2 - 3j$ is a root
then $f(2 - 3j) = 0$.

ii) $2 - 3$j is a root $\Rightarrow 2 + 3$j is also a root.

iii) Complex roots are always in conjugate pairs.
A cubic equation has exactly three roots and so it can either have three real roots or one real and two complex roots.
In this case there are two complex roots and so the third root must be real.

The following example shows you two different methods you can use to solve a polynomial equation, once you know one root.

EXAMPLE 2

Solve the equation $2z^3 - 5z^2 + 22z - 10 = 0$, given that $1 + 3j$ is a root.

SOLUTION

Method 1
You can use the factor theorem which you met in C1.

$1 + 3j$ is a root $\Rightarrow 1 - 3j$ is also a root.

> You can write down a 2nd root straight away, since complex roots come in conjugate pairs.

$1 + 3j$ and $1 - 3j$ are roots $\Rightarrow (z - (1 + 3j))$ and $(z - (1 - 3j))$ are factors.

> Remember the factor theorem states that if $z = \alpha$ is a root of a polynomial then $(z - \alpha)$ is a factor.

Multiply these two factors to find an expression for a quadratic factor:

$$(z - (1 + 3j))(z - (1 - 3j)) = (z - 1)^2 + 9$$
$$= z^2 - 2z + 10$$

> Take care with your signs:
> $(-3j) \times (3j) = -9j^2$
> $\qquad\qquad = 9$

So $z^2 - 2z + 10$ is a factor of $2z^3 - 5z^2 + 22z - 10 = 0$.

You can use inspection to find the third linear factor:

$$(z^2 - 2z + 10)(\ldots + \ldots) = 2z^3 - 5z^2 + 22z - 10$$
$$\Rightarrow (z^2 - 2z + 10)(2z - 1) = 2z^3 - 5z^2 + 22z - 10$$

> You can also use long division but inspection is quicker!

> The first term in this bracket is $2z$ since $z^2 \times 2z = 2z^3 \ldots$

$(2z - 1)$ is a factor $\Rightarrow z = \frac{1}{2}$ is a root.
So the roots are $z = 1 \pm 3j$ and $z = \frac{1}{2}$.

> … the second term is -1 since $+10 \times -1 = -10$

Method 2
You can use properties of the roots of polynomials which you met in FP1.

$1 + 3j$ is a root $\Rightarrow 1 - 3j$ is also a root.

> Look at the Key facts in 'Properties of the roots of polynomial equations' on page 51 to remind yourself of the root relationships.

So using sum of roots $= -\dfrac{b}{a}$ then:

$$(1 + 3j) + (1 - 3j) + \gamma = -\frac{-5}{2}$$
$$\Rightarrow 2 + \gamma = \frac{5}{2}$$
$$\Rightarrow \gamma = \frac{1}{2}$$

So the roots are $z = 1 \pm 3j$ or $z = \frac{1}{2}$.

> If α, β and γ are roots of $az^3 + bz^2 + cz + d = 0$ then $\sum \alpha = -\dfrac{b}{a}$ and $\alpha\beta\gamma = -\dfrac{d}{a}$.

> $b = -5$ and $a = 2$

> Or you could use product of roots $= -\dfrac{d}{a}$.

Sometimes you are given a root of a polynomial equation and are asked to use that root to find the missing coefficients in the equation.

EXAMPLE 3

$2 + j$ is a root of the equation $z^4 + pz^3 - 6z^2 + 22z + q = 0$ where p and q are real numbers.
Find the values of p and q.

SOLUTION

$z^2 = (2 + j)^2 = 4 + 4j - 1$
$= 3 + 4j$

$z^3 = z^2 \times z = (3 + 4j)(2 + j)$
$= 6 + 11j - 4$
$= 2 + 11j$

$z^4 = z^3 \times z = (2 + 11j)(2 + j)$
$= 4 + 24j - 11$
$= -7 + 24j$

Substitute above into $z^4 + pz^3 - 6z^2 + 22z + q = 0$
$\Rightarrow -7 + 24j + p(2 + 11j) - 6(3 + 4j) + 22(2 + j) + q = 0$

Tidying up: $-7 + 24j + 2p + 11pj - 18 - 24j + 44 + 22j + q = 0$
$(19 + 2p + q) + (22 + 11p)j = 0$

So $\quad 22 + 11p = 0$ ←
$\Rightarrow p = -2$

And $\quad 19 + 2p + q = 0$ ←
$19 - 4 + q = 0$
$\Rightarrow q = -15$

> Remember a complex number can only equal zero if both its real and **imaginary** parts are zero.

LINKS

Complex Numbers   FP2

Test Yourself

1 Which of the following statements are true for polynomials with real coefficients?

  I   A quartic equation can have exactly one complex root
  II A polynomial equation with odd degree must have at least one real root
  III A polynomial of degree n has n real roots.

  A **I** only
  B **II** only
  C **III** only

  D **I** and **III** only
  E **II** and **III** only

2 Given that a polynomial equation with real coefficients has one root of $-1 + 2j$, write down a second root.

  A $1 - 2j$

  B $-1 - 2j$

  C $1 + 2j$

  D You can't say without knowing the equation.

3 Which of these quadratic equations with real coefficients has $3 - 2j$ as a root?

  A $z^2 - 6z + 5 = 0$

  B $z^2 + 6z + 13 = 0$

  C $z^2 - 6z + 13 = 0$

  D $z^2 + 6z + 5 = 0$

4 You are given that $z = 2 + 4j$ satisfies the cubic equation $2z^3 + Az^2 + Bz - 60 = 0$, where A and B are real numbers.

Find the values of A and B.

A $A = -13$ and $B = 44$ **B** $A = -3$ and $B = -44$

C $A = -11$ and $B = 52$ **D** $A = \frac{55}{8}$ and $B = -\frac{167}{2}$

5 Solve the equation $z^4 - 5z^3 - 3z^2 + 19z - 30 = 0$ given that $2 - j$ is a root.

A $z = 2 \pm j$, $z = 3.70$ or $z = -2.70$ **B** $z = 2 \pm j$, $z = 3$ or $z = -2$

C $z = 2 \pm j$, $z = 0.62$ or $z = -9.62$ **D** $z = 2 \pm j$, $z = 6$ or $z = -1$

Exam-Style Question

The quartic equation $z^4 + Az^3 + Bz^2 + Cz + D = 0$, where A, B, C and D are real numbers, has roots $3 - j$ and $2j$.

i) Write down the other roots of the equation.

ii) Find the values of A, B, C and D.

Graphs and inequalities

3

Graphs of rational functions

A ABOUT THIS TOPIC

This topic is about sketching graphs of rational functions. Graph sketching is an important mathematical skill for showing how functions behave. It can also be used to help solve inequalities. Using sketch graphs to help solve inequalities is covered in the next topic.

R REMEMBER

- Algebra and curve sketching from C1.
- Curve sketching from C2.

K KEY FACTS

- A rational function can be written as one polynomial divided by another polynomial, that is $y = \dfrac{f(x)}{g(x)}$.

- In FP1 you will only meet rational functions in the form $y = \dfrac{f(x)}{g(x)}$, for which the degree of $g(x)$ is greater than or equal to the degree of $f(x)$. Such functions may have vertical and horizontal asymptotes.

- A vertical asymptote is a line parallel to the y axis (i.e. a line with equation $x = k$) that the graph of a function approaches but does not cross.

- The graph of a rational function $y = \dfrac{f(x)}{g(x)}$ has a vertical asymptote at $x = k$ if the function is undefined for $x = k$. This happens if $g(k) = 0$.

- A horizontal asymptote is a line parallel to the x axis (i.e. a line with equation $y = k$) that the graph of a function approaches as x becomes either very large and negative or very large and positive. The graph of a function may cross a horizontal asymptote.

- For a rational function $y = \dfrac{f(x)}{g(x)}$, if the degree of $g(x)$ is greater than the degree of $f(x)$, the graph of the function will have a horizontal asymptote at $y = 0$.

- For a rational function $y = \dfrac{f(x)}{g(x)}$, if the degree of $g(x)$ is equal to the degree of $f(x)$, and if the coefficient of the highest power of x in $f(x)$ is a, and the coefficient of the highest power of x in $g(x)$ is b, the graph of the function will have a horizontal asymptote at $y = \dfrac{a}{b}$.

Sketching graphs of rational functions

You can construct a sketch of a rational function by following a series of steps. These steps enable you to identify the key features of the function and illustrate them on a sketch which shows clearly how the function behaves.

Suppose you are asked to sketch the graph of $y = \dfrac{x(x+3)}{(2x+5)(x-4)}$.

Step 1 *Find where the curve crosses the x and y axes.*

When $x = 0$, $y = 0$, so the curve cuts the y axis at $(0, 0)$.

$y = 0$ when $x(x + 3) = 0$, so $x = 0$ or $x = -3$, so the curve cuts the x axis at $(0, 0)$ and $(-3, 0)$.

Step 2 *Find the equations of any vertical asymptotes and examine the sign of the function near them.*

$y = \dfrac{x(x+3)}{(2x+5)(x-4)}$ is undefined when $(2x+5)(x-4) = 0$, i.e. when $x = -\frac{5}{2}$ or $x = 4$, so the graph will have vertical asymptotes at $x = -\frac{5}{2}$ and $x = 4$.

A table will help you to decide how the graph of $y = \dfrac{x(x+3)}{(2x+5)(x-4)}$ approaches these asymptotes. As a graph approaches a vertical asymptote, it will either be large and positive, or large and negative.

	x slightly less than $-\frac{5}{2}$	x slightly greater than $-\frac{5}{2}$	x slightly less than 4	x slightly greater than 4
x	$-$	$-$	$+$	$+$
$(x+3)$	$+$	$+$	$+$	$+$
$(2x+5)$	$-$	$+$	$+$	$+$
$(x-4)$	$-$	$-$	$-$	$+$
$y = \dfrac{x(x+3)}{(2x+5)(x-4)}$	$\dfrac{(-)\times(+)}{(-)\times(-)}$ = negative. y large and negative just to the left of $x = -\frac{5}{2}$	$\dfrac{(-)\times(+)}{(+)\times(-)}$ = positive. y large and positive just to the right of $x = -\frac{5}{2}$	$\dfrac{(+)\times(+)}{(+)\times(-)}$ = negative. y large and negative just to the left of $x = 4$	$\dfrac{(+)\times(+)}{(+)\times(+)}$ = positive. y large and positive just to the right of $x = 4$

Step 3 *Find the equations of any horizontal asymptotes and, where a horizontal asymptote exists, determine whether the curve approaches it from above or below for large positive and large negative values of x.*

The degree of the 'top' of the algebraic fraction $y = \dfrac{x(x+3)}{(2x+5)(x-4)} = \dfrac{x^2+3x}{2x^2-3x-20}$ is the same as the degree of the 'bottom' of the algebraic fraction. As x gets very large, the terms in x^2, the highest power of x, will become far larger than the other terms and y will approach $y = \dfrac{x^2}{2x^2} = \dfrac{1}{2}$, so the graph will have a horizontal asymptote at $y = \frac{1}{2}$.

To find out how the curve approaches the horizontal asymptote for large positive and large negative values of x, at FP1 level it is acceptable to substitute in some values, say $x = 100$ and $x = -100$.

When $x = 100$, $y = \dfrac{x(x+3)}{(2x+5)(x-4)} = \dfrac{100 \times 103}{205 \times 96} = 0.523\ldots$

Since $0.523\ldots > \frac{1}{2}$, the curve approaches the horizontal asymptote from above for large positive values of x.

When $x = -100$, $y = \dfrac{x(x+3)}{(2x+5)(x-4)} = \dfrac{-100 \times -97}{-195 \times -104} = 0.478\ldots$

Since $0.478\ldots<\frac{1}{2}$, the curve approaches the horizontal asymptote from below for large negative values of x.

Step 4 *Construct a framework for your sketch, showing the asymptotes and the points where the curve crosses the axes, and then use the information about how the curve approaches the asymptotes to sketch in the branches of the curve.*

$y = \dfrac{x(x + 3)}{(2x + 5)(x - 4)}$ has two vertical asymptotes, so the curve will have three branches.

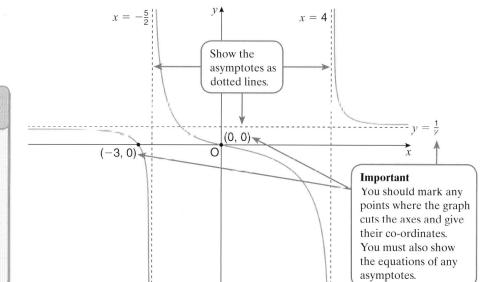

$x = -\frac{5}{2}$ $x = 4$

Show the asymptotes as dotted lines.

$y = \frac{1}{2}$

$(0, 0)$

$(-3, 0)$

O

A ADVICE

You are **sketching** the graph, not **plotting** it, so there is no need to use graph paper and the scale does not need to be accurate. However, it's a good idea to use a ruler to draw in the axes and the asymptotes.

Important
You should mark any points where the graph cuts the axes and give their co-ordinates. You must also show the equations of any asymptotes.

EXAMPLE 1

Sketch the graph of $y = \dfrac{x^2 - 2}{(x - 2)(x + 3)}$.

SOLUTION

Notice that the top of the algebraic fraction can be factorised as a difference of two squares.

Begin by finding where the curve crosses the axes.

$x^2 - 2 = (x + \sqrt{2})(x - \sqrt{2})$, so $y = 0$ when $x = \pm\sqrt{2}$, so the curve cuts the x axis at $(\sqrt{2}, 0)$ and $(-\sqrt{2}, 0)$.

When $x = 0$, $y = \dfrac{-2}{-2 \times 3} = \dfrac{1}{3}$, so the curve cuts the y axis at $\left(0, \frac{1}{3}\right)$.

$y = \dfrac{x^2 - 2}{(x - 2)(x + 3)}$ is undefined at $x = 2$ and $x = -3$, so the graph has vertical asymptotes at $x = 2$ and $x = -3$.

The graph of the function will have vertical asymptotes where the 'bottom' of the fraction equals 0.

	x just less than -3	x just greater than -3	x just less than 2	x just greater than 2
$x^2 - 2$	$+$	$+$	$+$	$+$
$(x - 2)$	$-$	$-$	$-$	$+$
$(x + 3)$	$-$	$+$	$+$	$+$
$y = \dfrac{x^2 - 2}{(x - 2)(x + 3)}$	$\dfrac{+}{(-) \times (-)} =$ positive	$\dfrac{+}{(-) \times (+)} =$ negative	$\dfrac{+}{(-) \times (+)} =$ negative	$\dfrac{+}{(+) \times (+)} =$ positive

Use a table to determine the sign of the function either side of the vertical asymptotes.

The degree of the 'top' of the algebraic fraction

$$y = \frac{x^2 - 2}{(x - 2)(x + 3)} = \frac{x^2 - 2}{x^2 + x - 6}$$ is the same as the degree of the 'bottom'

of the algebraic fraction. As x gets very large, the terms in x^2, the highest power of x, will become far larger than the other terms and y will approach $y = \frac{x^2}{x^2} = 1$ so the graph will have a horizontal asymptote at $y = 1$.

> Substitute in a large positive and a large negative value of x (± 100 is a good choice) to determine how the curve approaches the horizontal asymptote.

When $x = 100$, $y = \dfrac{x^2 - 2}{(x - 2)(x + 3)} = \dfrac{9998}{98 \times 103} = 0.990\ldots$

Since $0.990\ldots < 1$, the curve approaches the horizontal asymptote from below for large positive values of x.

When $x = -100$, $y = \dfrac{x^2 - 2}{(x - 2)(x + 3)} = \dfrac{9998}{-102 \times (-97)} = 1.010\ldots$

Since $1.010\ldots > 1$, the curve approaches the horizontal asymptote from above for large negative values of x.

> Clearly show approach to horizontal asymptote from above for this branch.

> Clearly show approach to horizontal asymptote from below for this branch.

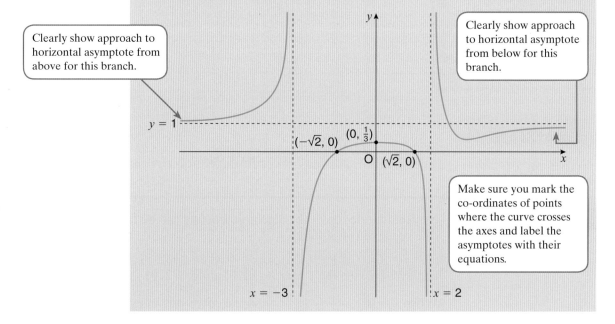

> Make sure you mark the co-ordinates of points where the curve crosses the axes and label the asymptotes with their equations.

IMPORTANT

If you graph rational functions on a graphical calculator the results can be misleading.

- Graphical calculators often do not deal with vertical asymptotes correctly.
- It can be very difficult to determine whether a curve shown on a graphical calculator display approaches a horizontal asymptote from above or below.

To draw a good sketch it is always best to analyse the function, as shown in these examples.

A copy of a graphical calculator display, without labelling or workings will not earn you marks in the examination.

EXAMPLE 2

Sketch the graph of $y = \dfrac{x}{(x-4)(1-x)}$.

SOLUTION

When $x = 0$, $y = 0$, so the curve cuts the axes at $(0, 0)$.

$y = \dfrac{x}{(x-4)(1-x)}$ is undefined for $x = 4$ and $x = 1$, so the graph has vertical asymptotes at $x = 4$ and $x = 1$.

	x just less than 1	x just greater than 1	x just less than 4	x just greater than 4
x	+	+	+	+
$(x-4)$	−	−	−	+
$(1-x)$	+	−	−	−
$y = \dfrac{x}{(x-4)(1-x)}$	$\dfrac{\mid}{(-)\times(+)} =$ negative	$\dfrac{\mid}{(-)\times(-)} =$ positive	$\dfrac{\mid}{(-)\times(-)} =$ positive	$\dfrac{\mid}{(+)\times(-)} =$ negative

The degree of the 'top' of the algebraic fraction

$y = \dfrac{x}{(x-4)(1-x)} = \dfrac{x}{-x^2 + 5x - 4}$ is less than the degree of the 'bottom'

of the algebraic fraction and the graph will have a horizontal asymptote at $y = 0$.

When $x = 100$, $y = \dfrac{x}{(x-4)(1-x)} = \dfrac{100}{96 \times (-99)} = -0.010\ldots$

Since $-0.010\ldots < 0$, the curve approaches the horizontal asymptote from below for large positive values of x.

When $x = -100$, $y = \dfrac{x}{(x-4)(1-x)} = \dfrac{-100}{-104 \times 101} = 0.009\ldots$

Since $0.009\ldots > 0$, the curve approaches the horizontal asymptote from above for large negative values of x.

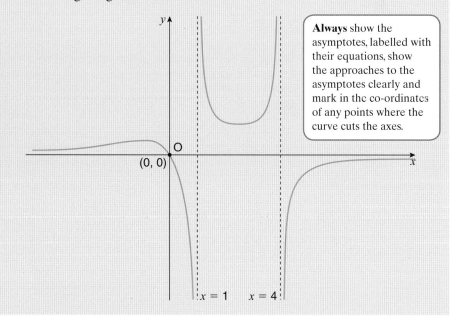

> **Always** show the asymptotes, labelled with their equations, show the approaches to the asymptotes clearly and mark in the co-ordinates of any points where the curve cuts the axes.

LINKS

Functions	C3
Hyperbolic Functions	FP2
Investigation of Curves	FP2

Test Yourself

1 The graph of $y = \dfrac{x^2 + 4}{(x - 3)(x + 4)}$ crosses the axes at

  A $(3, 0), (-4, 0)$ and $\left(0, -\frac{1}{3}\right)$ **B** $\left(0, -\frac{1}{3}\right)$ only

  C $(-3, 0), (4, 0)$ and $\left(0, -\frac{1}{3}\right)$ **D** $(2, 0), (-2, 0)$ and $\left(0, \frac{1}{3}\right)$

  E $\left(0, \frac{1}{3}\right)$ only

2 The graph of $y = \dfrac{3x^2 - 4}{(x + 5)(x - 3)}$ has asymptotes with equations

  A $y = \frac{4}{15}, x = 5$ and $x = -3$ **B** $y = 3, x = -5$ and $x = 3$

  C $y = 3, x = \dfrac{2}{\sqrt{3}}$ and $x = \dfrac{-2}{\sqrt{3}}$ **D** $y = 0, x = 5$ and $x = -3$

3 Which of the following statements about the graph of $y = \dfrac{3x}{x^2 - 5x + 6}$ are true?

  I   It has a horizontal asymptote at $y = 3$.

  II It has vertical asymptotes at $x = -2$ and $x = -3$.

  III It has a horizontal asymptote at $y = 0$.

  IV It cuts the x axis at $x = 0, x = 2$ and $x = 3$.

  V It has vertical asymptotes at $x = 2$ and $x = 3$.

  A **II** and **III**   **B** **II**, **III** and **IV**

  C **I**, **IV** and **V**   **D** **III** and **V**

  E **III**, **IV** and **V**

4 Which of the following could be a sketch of $y = \dfrac{(x^2 - 9)}{x(x + 2)(x - 1)}$?

A

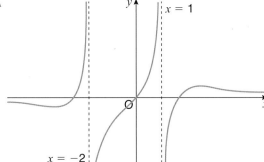

B

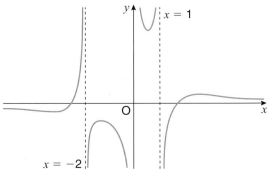

C

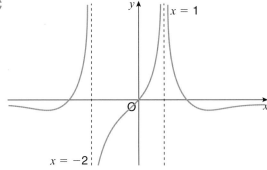

D

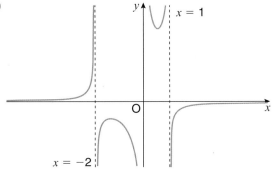

Exam-Style Question ▷L

A curve has equation $y = \dfrac{(2x - 3)(3x + 2)}{(2x - 1)(x + 2)}$.

i) Write down the co-ordinates of the points where the curve crosses the axes.

ii) Write down the equations of the three asymptotes.

iii) Determine whether the curve approaches the horizontal asymptote from above or below for
    A) large positive values of x.
    B) large negative values of x.

iv) Sketch the curve.

Inequalities

A ABOUT THIS TOPIC

This section is about solving inequalities involving rational functions.

R REMEMBER

- Solving linear and quadratic inequalities from C1.
- Curve sketching from C1 and C2.
- Graphs of rational functions from FP1 and the previous section of this Revise Guide.

K KEY FACTS

- The basic laws of inequalities:
  1 You may add or subtract the same number to or from both sides of an inequality,
    e.g. $x > y \Leftrightarrow x + a > y + a$.
  2 You may multiply or divide both sides of an inequality by the same positive number,
    e.g. if p is positive: $x > y \Leftrightarrow px > py$.
  3 If both sides of an inequality are multiplied or divided by the same negative number, the inequality is reversed,
    e.g. if n is negative: $x > y \Leftrightarrow nx < ny$.
  4 You may add, but not subtract, corresponding sides of inequalities of the same type,
    e.g. $a < b$ and $x < y \Rightarrow a + x < b + y$.
  5 Inequalities of the same type are *transitive*, e.g. $p < x$ and $x < y \Rightarrow p < y$.

Solving an inequality involving a rational function

The solutions to an inequality are the values of x for which the inequality is true. To find the solutions, you need to consider how the two sides of the inequality behave around the 'critical values'. The critical values are the values of x where the two sides of the inequality are equal, or where an expression involved in the inequality is undefined (this happens when the denominator of an expression equals 0). The critical values give the boundaries of the intervals where the solutions occur.

It is often easiest to solve an inequality involving a rational function by considering a sketch graph.

EXAMPLE 1

Solve the inequality $\dfrac{5}{x - 2} \geqslant 3$.

A ADVICE

Avoid multiplying both sides of an inequality by something that could be either positive or negative, because you will need to consider the positive and negative cases separately [see rules **2** and **3**], and it is easy to forget to do this. You can multiply both sides of an inequality by a square, because a square is always positive.

SOLUTION

Method 1

$$\frac{5}{x-2} \geqslant 3$$

> Multiply both sides of the inequality by $(x-2)^2$. This does not affect the inequality because $(x-2)^2$ must be positive [rule **2**].

$$\Rightarrow 5(x-2) \geqslant 3(x-2)^2$$
$$\Rightarrow 5x - 10 \geqslant 3x^2 - 12x + 12$$
$$\Rightarrow 0 \geqslant 3x^2 - 17x + 22$$
$$\Rightarrow 0 \geqslant (x-2)(3x-11)$$
$$\Rightarrow x = 2 \text{ and } x = \tfrac{11}{3} \text{ are the ciritical values, because the two sides of the}$$
inequality are equal for these values.

Now test some values either side of and in between the critical values:
Try $x < 2$, say $x = 1 \Rightarrow (x-2)(3x-11) = -1 \times -8 = 8$ and $0 < 8$.
Try $2 < x < \tfrac{11}{3}$, say $x = 3 \Rightarrow (x-2)(3x-11) = 1 \times -2 = -2$ and $0 > -2$.
Try $x > \tfrac{11}{3}$, say $x = 4 \Rightarrow (x-2)(3x-11) = 2 \times 1 = 2$ and $0 < 2$.
So, $0 \geqslant (x-2)(3x-11)$ for $2 \leqslant x \leqslant \tfrac{11}{3}$,

so $\frac{5}{x-2} \geqslant 3$ for $2 < x \leqslant \tfrac{11}{3}$.

>
> $\frac{5}{x-2}$ is undefined for $x = 2$, so $x = 2$ itself is not included in the solution.

Alternatively, to see where $0 \geqslant (x-2)(3x-11)$, it's easy to sketch a quick graph of $y = (x-2)(3x-11)$.

> Using the graph and the critical values, $0 \geqslant (x-2)(3x-11)$ for $2 \leqslant x \leqslant \tfrac{11}{3}$,
> so $\frac{5}{x-2} \geqslant 3$ for $2 < x \leqslant \tfrac{11}{3}$.

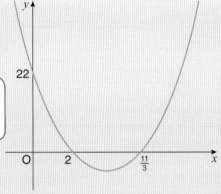

Method 2

Sketch graphs of $y = \frac{5}{x-2}$ and $y = 3$ on the same axes, identify the critical values, and read off the solution from the graph.

> At $x = 2$, $y = \frac{5}{x-2}$ is undefined, so $x = 2$ is a critical value, but is not part of the solution.

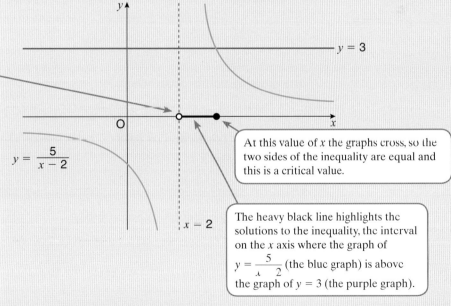

> At this value of x the graphs cross, so the two sides of the inequality are equal and this is a critical value.

> The heavy black line highlights the solutions to the inequality, the interval on the x axis where the graph of $y = \frac{5}{x-2}$ (the blue graph) is above the graph of $y = 3$ (the purple graph).

The crossing point occurs where $\frac{5}{x-2} = 3 \Rightarrow 3x - 11 = 0 \Rightarrow x = \tfrac{11}{3}$ and $y = \frac{5}{x-2}$ is undefined for $x = 2$. This means that the critical values are $x = 2$ and $x = \tfrac{11}{3}$.

Using the sketch graph and these critical values, and given that it is a 'greater than or equal to' inequality, the solution to the inequality $\dfrac{5}{x-2} \geqslant 3$ is $2 < x \leqslant \frac{11}{3}$.

EXAMPLE 2

Solve the inequality $\dfrac{1}{x-4} \leqslant x - 4$.

> This can be solved in a similar way to Method 1 of Example 1, but the method shown, using a sketch graph, is the easiest method.

SOLUTION

The solution will be the values of x for which the graph of $y = \dfrac{1}{x-4}$ is below the graph of $y = x - 4$. The inequality is 'less than or equal to', so the solution will include any points where the graphs cross. Both of these graphs are simple to sketch using techniques from C1 and C2.

> At $x = 4$,
> $$y = \frac{1}{x-4}$$
> is undefined, so $x = 4$ is a critical value, but is not part of the solution.

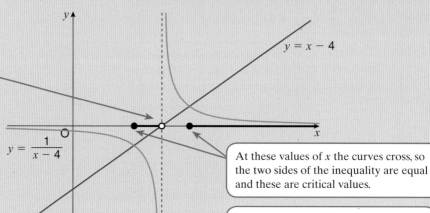

> At these values of x the curves cross, so the two sides of the inequality are equal and these are critical values.

> The heavy black lines highlight the solutions to the inequality, the intervals on the x axis where the graph of
> $$y = \frac{1}{x-4}$$
> (the blue graph) is below the graph of $y = x - 4$ (the purple graph).

The crossing points occur where

$$\dfrac{1}{x-4} = x - 4 \Rightarrow x^2 - 8x + 15 = 0 \Rightarrow (x-3)(x-5) = 0 \Rightarrow x = 3 \text{ or } x = 5$$

and $y = \dfrac{1}{x-4}$ is undefined for $x = 4$. This means that the critical values are $x = 3, x = 4$ and $x = 5$.

Using the sketch graph and these critical values, and given that it is a 'less than or equal to' inequality, the solution to the inequality $\dfrac{1}{x-4} \leqslant x - 4$ is $3 \leqslant x < 4$ or $x \geqslant 5$.

EXAMPLE 3

The graph below shows the rational function $y = \dfrac{3x^2 - 5}{x^2 - 4}$.

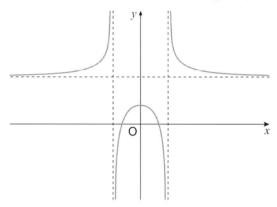

Solve the inequality $\dfrac{3x^2 - 5}{x^2 - 4} > 0$.

SOLUTION

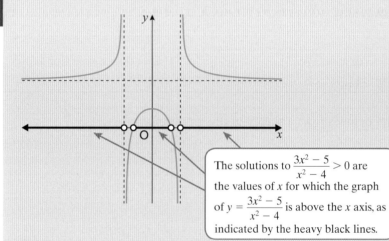

> The solutions to $\dfrac{3x^2 - 5}{x^2 - 4} > 0$ are the values of x for which the graph of $y = \dfrac{3x^2 - 5}{x^2 - 4}$ is above the x axis, as indicated by the heavy black lines.

$\dfrac{3x^2 - 5}{x^2 - 4} = 0 \Rightarrow 3x^2 - 5 = 0 \Rightarrow x = \sqrt{\tfrac{5}{3}} \text{ or } x = -\sqrt{\tfrac{5}{3}}$.

$y = \dfrac{3x^2 - 5}{x^2 - 4} = \dfrac{3x^2 - 5}{(x + 2)(x - 2)}$ is undefined for $x = 2$ and $x = -2$.

So the critical values are $x = \sqrt{\tfrac{5}{3}}, x = -\sqrt{\tfrac{5}{3}}, x = 2$ and $x = -2$.

From the graph, $\dfrac{3x^2 - 5}{x^2 - 4} > 0$ for $x < -2$,

> The inequality is 'greater than', so none of the critical values are included in the solution.

$-\sqrt{\tfrac{5}{3}} < x < \sqrt{\tfrac{5}{3}}$ and $x > 2$.

LINKS

Functions   C3

Test Yourself

1 One or more of the following statements about inequalities is false. Which statement(s) are false?

   I   If $x > y$ then $ax > ay$ for all values of a.

   II If $x > y$ then $x - s > y - s$ for all values of s.

   III If $x > y$ then $\dfrac{1}{x} > \dfrac{1}{y}$.

   IV $\dfrac{1}{x + 2} > x - 5 \Leftrightarrow 1 > (x - 5)(x + 2)$

   V $\dfrac{1}{x - 1} > x \Leftrightarrow x - 1 > x(x - 1)^2$

   A **I** and **III**   **B** **II** and **IV**   **C** **I**, **III** and **IV**

   D **V** only   **E** **II** and **V**

2 Solve the inequality $(x - 2)(2x - 1)(x + 4) \leqslant 0$.

   A $\frac{1}{2} \leqslant x \leqslant 2$ or $x \leqslant -4$ **B** $-4 \leqslant x \leqslant \frac{1}{2}$ or $x \geqslant 2$

   C $\frac{1}{2} < x < 2$ or $x < -4$ **D** $-4 < x < \frac{1}{2}$ or $x > 2$

3 Solve the inequality $\dfrac{6}{x + 3} \geqslant x - 2$.

   A $-4 \leqslant x \leqslant 3$ **B** $-3 < x \leqslant 3$ or $x \leqslant -4$

   C $-3 \leqslant x \leqslant 3$ or $x \leqslant -4$ **D** $-3 > x \geqslant -4$ or $x \geqslant 3$

   E $-3 \geqslant x \geqslant -4$ or $x \geqslant 3$

4 The diagram below shows a sketch of the graph of $y = \dfrac{x^2 - 4}{(5 - x)(x + 3)}$.

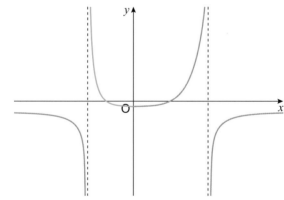

   Solve the inequality $\dfrac{x^2 - 4}{(5 - x)(x + 3)} < 0$.

   A $-2 < x < 2$ **B** $-3 < x < -2$ or $2 < x < 5$

   C $x < -3$, $-2 \leqslant x \leqslant 2$ or $x > 5$ **D** $x < -3$, $-2 < x < 2$ or $x > 5$

Exam-Style Question

Solve the inequality $\dfrac{2}{4 - x} \leqslant 5 - x$.

Algebra: identities and roots of equations

4

Identities

A ABOUT THIS TOPIC

An identity is a mathematical statement which says that two expressions are equal for all values of the variables. In an identity the symbol $\equiv$, which means 'is identically equal to', replaces the equals sign. In this section you will learn how to recognise an identity and how to find the values of constants in an identity.

R REMEMBER

- Knowing what an expression is from GCSE and C1.
- Knowing what an equation is from GCSE and C1.

K KEY FACTS

- The identity symbol is $\equiv$ and it is used to show an equation is true for all values of the variables.

You can connect two expressions using an '=' to make an **equation**.

An equation says that:

'two expressions are equal for one or more values of the variables.'

When the two expressions are equal for all values of the variables, you can replace '=' with the identity symbol $\equiv$, to make an **identity**.

An identity says that:

'two expressions are equal for **all** values of the variables.'

EXAMPLE 1

Which of the following are identities?

i) $x^2 + 2x - 3 = 0$

ii) $4x + 2y = 2(2x + y)$

iii) $\dfrac{1}{R_1} + \dfrac{1}{R_2} = \dfrac{R_1 + R_2}{R_1 R_2}$

SOLUTION

i) $x^2 + 2x - 3 = 0$ is an equation, not an identity. The equation is only true when $x = -3$ and $x = 1$. For all other values of x the equation is not true.

> For example, when $x = 2$ then $2^2 + 2 \times 2 - 3 \neq 0$

ii) $4x + 2y$ factorises to give $2(2x + y)$. So $4x + 2y = 2(2x + y)$ is an identity as it is true for all values of x and y. You can write it as $4x + 2y \equiv 2(2x + y)$.

SOLUTION

iii) $\dfrac{1}{R_1} + \dfrac{1}{R_2} = \dfrac{R_2}{R_1 R_2} + \dfrac{R_1}{R_1 R_2}$ ← Write both fractions with $R_1 R_2$ as a common denominator.

$\qquad\qquad = \dfrac{R_1 + R_2}{R_1 R_2}$

So you can write $\dfrac{1}{R_1} + \dfrac{1}{R_2} \equiv \dfrac{R_1 + R_2}{R_1 R_2}$ as the statement is true for all

values of R_1 and R_2, provided $R_1 \neq 0$ and $R_2 \neq 0$, as both sides of the identity are undefined for these values.

In the examination, you may be given the left hand side of an identity and asked to use it to complete the expression on the right hand side. The next example shows you two methods you can use to solve this type of problem.

EXAMPLE 2

Find the values of A, B and C in the identity
$5x^2 - 4x + 3 \equiv (Ax + B)(x - 1) + C$.

SOLUTION

Method 1

Comparing coefficients and the constant term

$5x^2 - 4x + 3 \equiv (Ax + B)(x - 1) + C$ ← Expand the brackets …

$\qquad\qquad\quad \equiv Ax^2 - Ax + Bx - B + C$ ← … combine like terms.

$\qquad\qquad\quad \equiv Ax^2 + (B - A)x - B + C$

Comparing coefficients of x^2: $5 = A$ ← Since the two expressions are equal for all values of x, the coefficients of x^2 must be the same on both sides …

Comparing coefficients of x: $B - A = -4 \Rightarrow B - 5 = -4$
$\qquad\qquad\qquad\qquad\qquad\quad \Rightarrow \qquad B = 1$

… and the coefficient of x must be the same …

Comparing constant terms: $-B + C = 3 \Rightarrow -1 + C = 3$
$\qquad\qquad\qquad\qquad\qquad\qquad\quad \Rightarrow \qquad C = 4$

So $A = 5$, $B = 1$ and $C = 4$ and
$5x^2 - 4x + 3 \equiv (5x + 1)(x - 1) + 4$.

… and likewise the constant term must be the same on both sides.

Method 2

Choosing values for x and substituting into the identity

$5x^2 - 4x + 3 \equiv (Ax + B)(x - 1) + C$

You can choose any three values of x and then solve the resulting simultaneous equations, but it is best to choose values of x that will eliminate some of the unknowns.

Substitute $x = 1$: $5 - 4 + 3 = C$ $\qquad\qquad \Rightarrow C = 4$

Substitute $x = 0$: $3 = -B + C$ $\qquad\qquad \Rightarrow 3 = -B + 4$
$\qquad\qquad\qquad\qquad\qquad\qquad\qquad\qquad\quad \Rightarrow B = 1$

Substitute $x = 2$: $20 - 8 + 3 = 2A + B + C \Rightarrow 15 = 2A + 1 + 4$
$\qquad\qquad\qquad\qquad\qquad\qquad\qquad\qquad\qquad\quad \Rightarrow A = 5$

So $A = 5$, $B = 1$ and $C = 4$ and
$5x^2 - 4x + 3 \equiv (5x + 1)(x - 1) + 4$.

In practice it can be more efficient to use a combination of these two methods.

EXAMPLE 3

Find the values of A, B, C and D in the identity
$$2x^3 - 1 \equiv (x + 1)(Ax^2 + Bx + C) + D.$$

SOLUTION

Equating coefficients of x^3: $\quad 2 = A \qquad \Rightarrow A = 2$

Substitute $x = -1$: $\qquad\qquad -3 = D \qquad \Rightarrow D = -3$

Substitute $x = 0$: $\qquad\qquad\;\; -1 = C + D \quad \Rightarrow -1 = C - 3$
$$\Rightarrow C = 2$$

Equating coefficients of x^2: $\quad 0 = A + B \quad \Rightarrow 0 = 2 + B$
$$\Rightarrow B = -2$$

> There is no x^2 term on the LHS so the coefficient is 0.

> On the RHS, the x^2 term is formed when the brackets are expanded: $1 \times Ax^2 + x \times Bx$.

LINKS

| Partial Fractions | C4 |
| Trigonometry | C4 |

Test Yourself

1 Which of these is an identity?

I $\quad 5a + b = 6ab$

II $\quad 9 - x^2 = (3 - x)(3 + x)$

III $\quad \dfrac{a + b}{ab} = \dfrac{1}{a} + \dfrac{1}{b}$

A **I** only $\qquad\qquad$ B **II** only $\qquad\qquad$ C **III** only

D **I** and **III** only $\qquad$ E **II** and **III** only

2 Which of these is **not** an identity?

I $\quad a^3 - b^3 = (a - b)(a^2 + ab + b^2)$

II $\quad x^2 - 4x + 5 = (x - 2)^2 + 1$

III $\quad \dfrac{x + 6}{x + 2} - 3$

A **I** only $\qquad\qquad$ B **II** only $\qquad\qquad$ C **III** only

D **II** and **III** only $\qquad$ E **I**, **II** and **III**

3 Find the values of the constants A and B in the following identity.

$$x^2 - 6x - 1 \equiv (x - A)^2 + B$$

A $A = -3$ and $B = -10$ $\qquad\qquad$ B $A = 3$ and $B = -10$

C $A = 3$ and $B = 8$ $\qquad\qquad\qquad$ D $A = 3$ and $B = -8$

4 Find the values of the constants A, B and C in the following identity.

$$-7x + 11 \equiv A(x - 2)^2 + B(x + 1)(x - 2) + C(x + 1)$$

A $A = 2, B = -2$ and $C = -1$ B $A = 2, B = 2$ and $C = -1$

C $A = 2, B = -2$ and $C = 1$ D $A = -2, B = -2$ and $C = -1$

5 Find the values of the constants A, B, C and D in the following identity.

$$x^3 - 8 \equiv (x - 1)(Ax^2 + Bx + C) + D$$

A $A = 1, B = 1, C = 1$ and $D = -9$ B $A = 1, B = -1, C = -1$ and $D = -7$

C $A = 1, B = 1, C = 1$ and $D = 0$ D $A = 1, B = 1, C = 1$ and $D = -7$

Exam-Style Question ⊃L

Find the values of the constants A, B, C and D in the identity

$$3x^3 - x^2 + 1 \equiv (x - 2)(Ax^2 + Bx + C) + D.$$

Properties of the roots of polynomial equations

A ABOUT THIS TOPIC

The sums and products of the roots of polynomial equations are related to the coefficients of the terms in the polynomial. In this topic, you use and manipulate these relationships in order to either find a polynomial whose roots have certain properties, or to find a polynomial whose roots are related to the roots of another polynomial.

R REMEMBER

- Solving quadratic equations from GCSE and C1.
- Transformations of graphs from GCSE.
- Polynomials from C1.
- Binomial expansions from C1.

K KEY FACTS

- For a quadratic equation $az^2 + bz + c = 0$, with roots α and β:

$$\alpha + \beta = -\frac{b}{a}$$

and $\quad \alpha\beta = \frac{c}{a}$

- For a cubic equation $az^3 + bz^2 + cz + d = 0$, with roots α, β and γ:

$$\sum\alpha = \alpha + \beta + \gamma = -\frac{b}{a}$$

$$\sum\alpha\beta = \alpha\beta + \beta\gamma + \gamma\alpha = \frac{c}{a}$$

and $\quad \alpha\beta\gamma = -\frac{d}{a}$

- For a quartic equation $az^4 + bz^3 + cz^2 + dz + e = 0$, with roots α, β, γ and δ:

$$\sum\alpha = \alpha + \beta + \gamma + \delta = -\frac{b}{a}$$

$$\sum\alpha\beta = \alpha\beta + \alpha\gamma + \beta\delta + \beta\gamma + \gamma\delta + \delta\alpha = \frac{c}{a}$$

$$\sum\alpha\beta\gamma = \alpha\beta\gamma + \beta\gamma\delta + \gamma\delta\alpha + \delta\alpha\beta = -\frac{d}{a}$$

and $\quad \alpha\beta\gamma\delta = \frac{e}{a}$

The sums and products of the roots of a polynomial equation are related to the coefficients and the constant term in the polynomial. For example, for a quadratic equation, $az^2 + bz + c = 0$, with roots α and β, then:

The sum of the roots. $\longrightarrow \quad \alpha + \beta = -\dfrac{b}{a} \quad$ The product of the roots.

and $\quad \alpha\beta = \dfrac{c}{a} \quad$ See 'Complex numbers and equations', page 31.

These properties apply even when the quadratic has complex roots and, to remind you of this, the variable is often written as z rather than x.

4 Algebra: identities and roots of equations

EXAMPLE 1

The roots of the quadratic equation $3x^2 - 6x + 4 = 0$ are α and β.

i) Find the values of $\alpha\beta$ and $\alpha + \beta$.

ii) Hence find the value of $\alpha^2 + \beta^2$.

SOLUTION

i) $3x^2 - 6x + 4 = 0 \Rightarrow a = 3, b = -6$ and $c = 4$

$\alpha + \beta = -\dfrac{b}{a} \Rightarrow \alpha + \beta = -\dfrac{-6}{3} = 2$

$\alpha\beta = \dfrac{c}{a} \Rightarrow \alpha\beta = \dfrac{4}{3}$

ii) You can use the fact that $(\alpha + \beta)^2 = \alpha^2 + 2\alpha\beta + \beta^2$ ①

From part i) $\alpha + \beta = 2 \Rightarrow (\alpha + \beta)^2 = 4$ ②

and $\alpha\beta = \dfrac{4}{3} \Rightarrow 2\alpha\beta = \dfrac{8}{3}$ ③

Substituting ② and ③ into ① gives:

$$4 = \alpha^2 + \frac{8}{3} + \beta^2$$

$$\Rightarrow \alpha^2 + \beta^2 = \frac{4}{3}$$

In the same way, a cubic equation, $az^3 + bz^2 + cz + d = 0$ has roots α, β and γ with these properties:

Sum of roots $\longrightarrow$ $\sum\alpha = \alpha + \beta + \gamma = -\dfrac{b}{a}$

Product of roots in pairs

$\sum\alpha\beta = \alpha\beta + \beta\gamma + \gamma\alpha = \dfrac{c}{a}$

and $\alpha\beta\gamma = -\dfrac{d}{a}$ $\longleftarrow$ Product of roots

You can use these results to solve problems involving cubic equations.

EXAMPLE 2

The roots of the cubic equation $2x^3 + 5x^2 + px + q = 0$ are $\alpha, \dfrac{\alpha}{2}$ and $\alpha + 5$.

Find the values of α, p and q.

SOLUTION

$2x^3 + 5x^2 + px + q = 0$ has roots $\alpha, \dfrac{\alpha}{2}$ and $\alpha + 5$.

Sum of roots $= -\dfrac{b}{a} \Rightarrow \alpha + \left(\dfrac{\alpha}{2}\right) + (\alpha + 5) = -\dfrac{5}{2}$

From the cubic equation: $a = 2$ and $b = 5$.

$\Rightarrow \dfrac{5\alpha}{2} + 5 = -\dfrac{5}{2}$

$\Rightarrow \dfrac{5\alpha}{2} = -\dfrac{15}{2}$

$\Rightarrow \alpha = -3$

From the cubic equation: $a = 2$ and replace c with p.

The roots are $\alpha, \dfrac{\alpha}{2}$ and $\alpha + 5 \Rightarrow$ roots are $-3, -\dfrac{3}{2}$ and 2

The product of the roots in pairs $= \dfrac{c}{a}$

$$\Rightarrow (-3) \times \left(-\dfrac{3}{2}\right) + \left(-\dfrac{3}{2}\right) \times 2 + 2 \times (-3) = \dfrac{p}{2}$$

$$\Rightarrow \dfrac{9}{2} - 3 - 6 = \dfrac{p}{2}$$

$$\Rightarrow p = -9$$

The product of the roots $= -\dfrac{d}{a}$

> From the cubic equation:
> $a = 2$ and replace d with q.

$$\Rightarrow (-3) \times \left(-\frac{3}{2}\right) \times 2 = -\frac{q}{2}$$

$$\Rightarrow -9 = \frac{q}{2}$$

$$\Rightarrow q = -18$$

So the cubic equation is $2x^3 + 5x^2 - 9x - 18 = 0$ and $\alpha = -3$.

You can use the properties of roots to form a polynomial whose roots are related to the roots of another polynomial. For example, you might be asked to find a quadratic which has roots that are double the roots of another quadratic.

Here are two different methods you can use to solve this type of problem.

EXAMPLE 3

The roots of the cubic equation $2x^3 + x^2 - 5x + 2 = 0$ are α, β and γ.

Find a cubic equation whose roots are $2\alpha, 2\beta$ and 2γ.

SOLUTION

Method 1   *Transform the polynomial by using a suitable substitution*

Let $w = 2x \Rightarrow x = \dfrac{w}{2}$

> You are transforming the function $f(x)$ to $f\left(\frac{x}{2}\right)$ which is a one-way stretch parallel to the x axis, scale factor 2. So the roots of $f\left(\frac{x}{2}\right) = 0$ will be double the roots of $f(x) = 0$.

The roots of $2x^3 + x^2 - 5x + 2 = 0$ are α, β and γ

$\Rightarrow$ the roots of $2\left(\dfrac{w}{2}\right)^3 + \left(\dfrac{w}{2}\right)^2 - 5\left(\dfrac{w}{2}\right) + 2 = 0$ are $2\alpha, 2\beta$ and 2γ.

> Note
> $\left(\dfrac{w}{2}\right)^3 = \dfrac{w^3}{8}$

$\Rightarrow 2\left(\dfrac{w^3}{8}\right) + \dfrac{w^2}{4} - 5\left(\dfrac{w}{2}\right) + 2 = 0$

$\Rightarrow w^3 + w^2 - 10w + 8 = 0$

> Multiply each term by 4.

So the cubic $w^3 + w^2 - 10w + 8 = 0$ or $x^3 + x^2 - 10x + 8 = 0$ has roots $2\alpha, 2\beta$ and 2γ.

Method 2   *Use the properties of the roots*

$2x^3 + x^2 - 5x + 2 = 0 \Rightarrow a = 2, b = 1, c = -5$ and $d = 2$

Using the properties of the roots:

$$\sum \alpha = \alpha + \beta + \gamma = -\frac{1}{2} \qquad ①$$

$$\sum \alpha\beta = \alpha\beta + \beta\gamma + \gamma\alpha = -\frac{5}{2} \qquad ②$$

and $\quad \alpha\beta\gamma = -1 \qquad ③$

For the new cubic equation $Ax^3 + Bx^2 + Cx + D = 0$, the roots are $2\alpha, 2\beta$ and 2γ.

Using the sum of roots $= -\dfrac{B}{A}$

$$\Rightarrow 2\alpha + 2\beta + 2\gamma = 2(\alpha + \beta + \gamma) = -\frac{B}{A}$$

Substituting in ① gives: the sum of roots $= 2 \times \left(-\dfrac{1}{2}\right) = -1 = -\dfrac{B}{A}$

Letting $A = 1$ gives $B = 1$

Using the product of roots in pairs $= \dfrac{C}{A}$

$$\Rightarrow 2\alpha \times 2\beta + 2\beta \times 2\gamma + 2\gamma \times 2\alpha = 4(\alpha\beta + \beta\gamma + \gamma\alpha) = \dfrac{C}{A}$$

Substituting in ② gives: the product of roots in pairs $= 4\left(-\dfrac{5}{2}\right) = -10 = \dfrac{C}{A}$

$$\Rightarrow C = -10 \text{ since } A = 1$$

Using the product of roots $= -\dfrac{D}{A}$

$$\Rightarrow 2\alpha \times 2\beta \times 2\gamma = 8\alpha\beta\gamma = -\dfrac{D}{A}$$

Substituting in ③ gives: the product of roots $= 8 \times (-1) = -8 = -\dfrac{D}{A}$

$$\Rightarrow D = 8 \text{ since } A = 1$$

$A = 1, B = 1, C = -10$ and $D = 8$
$\Rightarrow$ the new cubic equation is $x^3 + x^2 - 10x + 8 = 0$

You can also extend these properties to quartic equations.

For the quartic equation $az^4 + bz^3 + cz^2 + dz + e = 0$ with roots α, β, γ and δ:

$$\sum\alpha = \alpha + \beta + \gamma + \delta = -\dfrac{b}{a}$$

$$\sum\alpha\beta = \alpha\beta + \alpha\gamma + \beta\delta + \beta\gamma + \gamma\delta + \delta\alpha = \dfrac{c}{a}$$

$$\sum\alpha\beta\gamma = \alpha\beta\gamma + \beta\gamma\delta + \gamma\delta\alpha + \delta\alpha\beta = -\dfrac{d}{a}$$

and $\quad \alpha\beta\gamma\delta = \dfrac{e}{a}$

LINKS

Complex Numbers	FP1
Transformations of Functions	C3

Test Yourself ▶L

1 A cubic equation has roots α, β and γ where

$$\alpha + \beta + \gamma = 4$$
$$\alpha\beta + \beta\gamma + \gamma\alpha = -\tfrac{3}{2}$$
and $$\alpha\beta\gamma = -2$$

Find the cubic equation.

A $2x^3 - 8x^2 - 3x + 4 = 0$ B $x^3 - 4x^2 - \tfrac{3}{2}x + 2$

C $2x^3 - 4x^2 - 3x + 2 = 0$ D $2x^3 + 8x^2 + 3x - 4 = 0$

2 The cubic equation $x^3 + 2x^2 - 3x + 4 = 0$ has roots α, β and γ.
Find the value of $\alpha^2 + \beta^2 + \gamma^2$.

A 4   B 2   C 10   D −2

3 The cubic equation $4x^3 - 12x^2 + px + q = 0$ has roots $\alpha, 2\alpha$ and $\alpha + 1$.
  Find the values of α, p and q.

A $\alpha = \frac{1}{2}, p = \frac{11}{8}$ and $q = -\frac{3}{8}$

B $\alpha = \frac{1}{2}, p = 11$ and $q = 3$

C $\alpha = \frac{11}{4}, p = 46.0625$ and $q = 56.71875$

D $\alpha = \frac{1}{2}, p = 11$ and $q = -3$

4 The roots of the quadratic equation $2x^2 + 3x - 1 = 0$ are α and β.
  Find a quadratic equation with roots $2\alpha + 1$ and $2\beta + 1$.

A $4x^2 + 6x - 1 = 0$

B $x^2 - x - 4 = 0$

C $x^2 + x - 4 = 0$

D $w^2 + w - 3 = 0$

E $4w^2 + 4w + 1 = 0$

5 The roots of the quartic equation $2x^4 - 5x^3 + 5x - 2 = 0$ are α, β, γ and δ.
  Use a suitable substitution to find a quartic equation whose roots are $2\alpha, 2\beta, 2\gamma$ and 2δ.

A $x^4 - 5x^3 + 20x = 0$

B $x^4 - 5x^3 + 20x - 16 = 0$

C $4x^4 - 10x^3 + 10x - 4 = 0$

D $16x^4 - 20x^3 + 5x - 1 = 0$

Exam-Style Question ▷L

The cubic equation $x^3 + 2x^2 - 3x + 4 = 0$ has roots α, β and γ.
i) Write down the values of $\alpha + \beta + \gamma, \alpha\beta + \beta\gamma + \gamma\alpha$ and $\alpha\beta\gamma$.
ii) Find the cubic equation with roots $\alpha + 1, \beta + 1$ and $\gamma + 1$.

Proof by induction

▶▶ 116
122

A ABOUT THIS TOPIC

Proof by induction is a way to prove that certain types of mathematical statement are true. Using proof by induction, it is possible to prove that a statement is true for infinitely many values of one of the integer variables it contains. An example of this is the statement $1^3 + 2^3 + 3^3 + \dots + n^3 = \frac{1}{4}n^2(n + 1)^2$. Proof by induction can be used to show that this is true for **all** positive integers $n = 1, 2, 3, 4, \dots$.

R REMEMBER

- Algebra from C1.
- Sigma notation from C2.

K KEY FACTS

- By using proof by induction, it is possible to prove that a statement is true for infinitely many whole numbers.
- Proof by induction is a structured logical argument. It can be used to prove mathematical statements about the integers.
- A proof by induction can be structured in four distinct steps, where n is a whole number:
  Step 1 Check that the statement you are trying to prove is true for the first case, $n = p$ (usually $p = 1$).
  Step 2 Assume that it is true for the general case, $n = k$.
  Step 3 Show that if it is true for $n = k$, it must also be true for $n = k + 1$.
  Step 4 Conclude your argument by stating that you have shown that if the statement is true for $n = k$, it is also true for $n = k + 1$ and that since it is also true for the first case, it is true for all integers greater than or equal to the first case.

Proof by induction

Suppose you are asked to prove that $\displaystyle\sum_{r=1}^{n} r^2 = \frac{1}{6}n(n + 1)(2n + 1)$ is true

for all positive integers n. You can check that it is true when $n = 1$, $n = 2$, $n = 3$ and so on just by substituting these values for n, but you could never prove it for **all** positive integers this way; there are infinitely many of them!

You can, however, prove it for all positive integers using a structured, logical argument called 'proof by induction'.

Step 1 Show that the statement is true when $n = 1$:

When $n = 1$, the left hand side is $\displaystyle\sum_{r=1}^{1} r^2 = 1^2 = 1$. Substituting $n = 1$ into

the right hand side, $\frac{1}{6}n(n + 1)(2n + 1)$, gives
$\frac{1}{6} \times 1 \times (1 + 1) \times (2 \times 1 + 1) = \frac{1}{6} \times 1 \times 2 \times 3 = 1$.

So, when $n = 1$, the left hand side and right hand side are equal and the statement is true.

Step 2 Assume that the statement is true for $n = k$, a positive integer,

so $\sum_{r=1}^{k} r^2 = \frac{1}{6}k(k + 1)(2k + 1)$. Notice that this is just the statement you are trying to prove but with n replaced by k.

Step 3 Show that if the assumption is true, so the statement is true when $n = k$, it will also be true when $n = k + 1$.

> At this point it is highly advisable to think about your **target**, which is the statement you are trying to prove but with n replaced by $k + 1$. Here you are trying to prove that
>
> $$\sum_{r=1}^{n} r^2 = \frac{1}{6}n(n + 1)(2n + 1).$$ By replacing every n with $k + 1$ and simplifying you get
>
> $$\sum_{r=1}^{k+1} r^2 = \frac{1}{6}(k + 1)((k + 1) + 1)(2(k + 1) + 1) = \frac{1}{6}(k + 1)(k + 2)(2k + 3).$$
>
> This is your **target**. This is what you need to show is true in **Step 3**. Look carefully at the above and make sure you understand how it's been obtained; it is very important.

If the statement is true when $n = k$, then

$$\sum_{r=1}^{k+1} r^2 = \left(\sum_{r=1}^{k} r^2\right) + (k + 1)^2 = \frac{1}{6}k(k + 1)(2k + 1) + (k + 1)^2.$$

> Adding the $(k + 1)$th term, $(k + 1)^2$, to both sides of the equation that you have assumed is true in Step 2.

$$\Rightarrow \sum_{r=1}^{k+1} r^2 = \frac{1}{6}k(k + 1)(2k + 1) + (k + 1)^2$$

> Now remember your target. You want to show that this is the same as $\frac{1}{6}(k + 1)(k + 2)(2k + 3)$.

$$= \frac{1}{6}(k + 1)[k(2k + 1) + 6(k + 1)]$$

> From your target, you can see it makes sense to use $\frac{1}{6}(k + 1)$ as a factor.

$$= \frac{1}{6}(k + 1)[2k^2 + 7k + 6]$$

> From your target, you can see it makes sense to factorise $(2k^2 + 7k + 6)$.

$$= \frac{1}{6}(k + 1)(k + 2)(2k + 3)$$

$$= \frac{1}{6}(k + 1)((k + 1) + 1)(2(k + 1) + 1)$$

> Expressing $(k + 2)$ as $((k + 1) + 1)$ and $(2k + 3)$ as $(2(k + 1) + 1)$ makes it absolutely clear that you have reached your target, which is the statement you are trying to prove, but with $k + 1$ replacing n

Step 4 Conclude your argument by explaining its logical structure:

So if the statement is true for $n = k$, it has been shown that it must also be true for $n = k + 1$. Since it has been shown to be true for $n = 1$, it must be true for all positive integers.

EXAMPLE 1	Prove by induction that $5 + 8 + 11 + \ldots + (3n + 2) = \frac{1}{2}n(3n + 7)$ is true for all positive integers n.

This could be proved in other ways, but if you are asked in an exam to prove something by induction, you must use proof by induction to earn any marks.

SOLUTION

The left hand side of this equation is the series $5 + 8 + 11 + \ldots + (3n + 2)$. When $n = 1$ the series has only one term and equals 5. Substituting $n = 1$ into the right hand side, $\frac{1}{2}n(3n + 7)$, gives $\frac{1}{2} \times 1 \times (3 \times 1 + 7) = 5$. So, when $n = 1$, the left hand side and right hand side of the statement are equal and the statement is true.

Assume the statement is true when $n = k$, a positive integer, so $5 + 8 + 11 + \ldots + (3k + 2) = \frac{1}{2}k(3k + 7)$.

Now think about your **target**, which is the statement you are trying to prove but with n replaced by $k + 1$. You are trying to prove that $5 + 8 + 11 + \ldots + (3n + 2) = \frac{1}{2}n(3n + 7)$. By replacing every n with $k + 1$ and simplifying you get (notice the extra term in the summation)

$$5 + 8 + 11 + \ldots + (3k + 2) + (3(k + 1) + 2)$$
$$= \frac{1}{2}(k + 1)(3(k + 1) + 7))$$
$$= \frac{1}{2}(k + 1)(3k + 10).$$

This is your target. Look carefully at the above and make sure you understand how it's been obtained.

So, to show that the target is true

$$5 + 8 + 11 + \ldots + (3k + 2) + (3(k + 1) + 2)$$

$$= [5 + 8 + 11 + \ldots + (3k + 2)] + (3k + 5)$$

Here the square brackets contain the sum of the first k terms of the series. You are working under the assumption that the formula for this is $\frac{1}{2}k(3k + 7)$ so you can replace the expression in square brackets with this.

$$= \frac{1}{2}k(3k + 7) + (3k + 5)$$

$$= \frac{1}{2}[k(3k + 7) + 6k + 10]$$

The target has a factor of $\frac{1}{2}$, so it makes sense to take out $\frac{1}{2}$ as a factor.

$$= \frac{1}{2}[3k^2 + 13k + 10]$$

Factorise the quadratic.

$$= \frac{1}{2}(k + 1)(3k + 10)$$

$$= \frac{1}{2}(k + 1)(3(k + 1) + 7)$$

Finish off by writing $(3k + 10)$ as $(3(k + 1) + 7)$ as in the target.

So if the statement is true for $n = k$, it has been shown that it must also be true for $n = k + 1$. Since it has been shown to be true for $n = 1$, it must be true for all positive integers.

You must show all the steps clearly, including the explanation and conclusion, to give a complete proof.

EXAMPLE 2

A sequence is defined by $a_1 = 7$ and $a_{k+1} = 7a_k - 3$. Prove by induction that $a_n = \dfrac{(13 \times 7^{n-1}) + 1}{2}$.

Note $7^{1-1} = 7^0 = 1$

SOLUTION

Substituting $n = 1$ into $\dfrac{(13 \times 7^{n-1}) + 1}{2}$ gives $\dfrac{(13 \times 7^{1-1}) + 1}{2} = \dfrac{13 + 1}{2} = 7.$

Since $a_1 = 7$, the statement is true when $n = 1$.

Assume the statement is true when $n = k$, a positive integer, so

$$a_k = \frac{(13 \times 7^{k-1}) + 1}{2}.$$

Find your target by substituting $n = k + 1$ into the statement you are trying

to prove. You are trying to prove that $a_n = \dfrac{(13 \times 7^{n-1}) + 1}{2}$. By replacing

every n with $k + 1$ and simplifying you get

$$a_{k+1} = \frac{(13 \times 7^{(k+1)-1}) + 1}{2} = \frac{(13 \times 7^{k}) + 1}{2}.$$

This is your target. Look carefully at the above and make sure you understand how it's been obtained.

Now

$$a_{k+1} = 7a_k - 3$$

> You need to express a_{k+1} in terms of a_k. You were told how to do this in the question.

> Here you use $a_k = \dfrac{(13 \times 7^{k-1}) + 1}{2}$.

$$= 7\left(\frac{(13 \times 7^{k-1}) + 1}{2}\right) - 3$$

> Be careful with your algebra here. Remember $7^{k-1} \times 7 = 7^k$.

$$= \frac{(13 \times 7^{k}) + 7}{2} - 3$$

> Your target is a fraction over 2, so write this whole expression as a fraction over 2.

$$= \frac{(13 \times 7^{k}) + 7}{2} - \frac{6}{2}$$

$$= \frac{(13 \times 7^{k}) + 1}{2}$$

> This is your target. Write k as $(k + 1) - 1$ to emphasise that this is the statement you are trying to prove with n replaced by $k + 1$.

$$= \frac{(13 \times 7^{(k+1)-1}) + 1}{2}$$

This shows that if the statement is true when $n = k$, it will also be true when $n = k + 1$.

So it has been shown that if the result is true for $n = k$, then it is true for $n = k + 1$. Since it has been shown to be true for $n = 1$, it must be true for all positive integers.

EXAMPLE 3   Prove by induction that $\displaystyle\sum_{r=1}^{n} 3^{r-1} = \frac{3^n - 1}{2}.$

SOLUTION

When $n = 1$, the left hand side is $\displaystyle\sum_{r=1}^{1} 3^{r-1} = 3^{1-1} = 3^0 = 1$.

Substituting $n = 1$ into the right hand side, $\dfrac{3^n - 1}{2}$, gives $\dfrac{3^1 - 1}{2} = \dfrac{2}{2} = 1$.

So the statement is true when $n = 1$.

Assume the statement is true when $n = k$, a positive integer, so

$$\sum_{r=1}^{k} 3^{r-1} = \frac{3^k - 1}{2}.$$

Find your target by substituting $n = k + 1$ into the statement that you are trying to prove.

You are trying to prove that $\sum_{r=1}^{n} 3^{r-1} = \dfrac{3^n - 1}{2}$. By replacing every n with $k + 1$ you get

$$\sum_{r=1}^{k+1} 3^{r-1} = \frac{3^{k+1} - 1}{2}.$$

This is your target.

Now

$$\sum_{r=1}^{k+1} 3^{r-1} = \left(\sum_{r=1}^{k} 3^{r-1} \right) + 3^k$$

> The final term in the sum $\sum_{r=1}^{k+1} 3^{r-1}$ is $3^{k+1-1} = 3^k$.

> You are working under the assumption that $\sum_{r=1}^{k} 3^{r-1} = \dfrac{3^k - 1}{2}$ and you use that here.

$$= \frac{3^k - 1}{2} + 3^k$$

$$= \frac{3^k - 1 + 2 \times 3^k}{2} = \frac{3 \times 3^k - 1}{2} = \frac{3^{k+1} - 1}{2}$$

> Look at your target to see where to go here. In this example you need to be careful with indices. Note: $3^k + 2 \times 3^k = 3 \times 3^k = 3^{k+1}$.

This shows that if the statement is true when $n = k$, it will also be true when $n = k + 1$.

So it has been shown that if the result is true for $n = k$, then it is true for $n = k + 1$. Since it has been shown to be true for $n = 1$, it must be true for all positive integers.

LINKS

Proof is fundamental to all of mathematics. The technique of proof by induction can be used to prove key results in topics in FP2 and FP3.

Test Yourself ⟩L

Look at the proof below, by induction, that $\sum_{r=1}^{n} r^3 = \frac{1}{4}n^2(n + 1)^2$.

Proof

When $n = 1$, the left hand side is $\sum_{r=1}^{1} r^3 = 1^3 = 1$.

Substituting $n = 1$ into the right hand side, $\frac{1}{4}n^2(n + 1)^2$, gives $\frac{1}{4}[1^2 \times (1 + 1)^2] = \frac{1}{4} \times 4 = 1$.

So the statement is true when $n = 1$.

Assume the statement is true when $n = k$, a positive integer, so .... Gap 1 .... $= \frac{1}{4}k^2(k + 1)^2$.

Working under this assumption it must be shown that the statement is true when $n = k + 1$, in other

words that $\sum_{r=1}^{k+1} r^3 = $ .... Gap 2 .... This is the **target**.

Now

$$\sum_{r=1}^{k+1} r^3 = \left(\sum_{r=1}^{k} r^3\right) + \boxed{\text{Gap 3}} \dots\dots\dots\dots\dots$$

This equals

$$= \tfrac{1}{4}k^2(k+1)^2 + (k+1)^3$$

$$\boxed{\text{Gap 4}}$$

$$= \tfrac{1}{4}(k+1)^2(k^2 + \dots\dots\dots\dots\dots\dots)$$
$$= \tfrac{1}{4}(k+1)^2(k^2 + 4k + 4)$$

$$\boxed{\text{Gap 5}}$$

$$= \tfrac{1}{4}(k+1)^2 \dots\dots\dots\dots\dots\dots$$
$$= \tfrac{1}{4}(k+1)^2((k+1)+1)^2$$

This shows that if the statement is true when $n = k$, it will also be true when $n = k + 1$.

So we have shown that if the result is true for $n = k$, then it is true for $n = k + 1$. Since it has been shown to be true for $n = 1$, it must be true for all positive integers.

1 What is missing from **Gap 1**?

A $\displaystyle\sum_{r=1}^{k} r^3$ B $\displaystyle\sum_{r=1}^{k+1} r^3$ C $\displaystyle\sum_{r=1}^{n} r^3$ D $\displaystyle\sum_{r=1}^{n+1} r^3$

2 What is missing from **Gap 2**?

A $\tfrac{1}{4}k^2(k+1)^2$ B $\tfrac{1}{4}(k+1)^2(k+2)^2$ C $\tfrac{1}{4}k^2(k+2)^2$ D $\tfrac{1}{4}(k+1)^2(k+1)^2$

3 What is missing from **Gap 3**?

A k B k^3 C $k+1$ D $(k+1)^3$

4 What is missing from **Gap 4**?

A $4(k+1)^3$ B $(k+1)^3$ C $k+1$ D $4(k+1)$

5 What is missing from **Gap 5**?

A $(k+2)^2$ B $(k+1)(k+2)$ C $(k+1)(k+4)$ D $(k+1)^2$

Exam-Style Question

Prove by induction that $\displaystyle\sum_{r=1}^{n} r2^{r-1} = 1 + (n-1)2^n$.

Summation of finite series

This section involves two techniques for finding formulae for the sum of certain types of finite series.

1 Using standard formulae for $\sum_{r=1}^{n} r, \sum_{r=1}^{n} r^2$ and $\sum_{r=1}^{n} r^3$ to find formulae for related summations.

2 The 'method of differences' which involves writing each term in a given summation as an expression involving subtraction. When the whole summation is written out like this you can cancel many terms across the whole sum, leaving a relatively simple final formula for the sum.

- Sigma notation and series from C2.
- Sequences from C2.
- Algebra from C1.

1 Using standard formulae

- The following are standard formulae.

$$\sum_{r=1}^{n} r = \tfrac{1}{2}n(n+1); \quad \sum_{r=1}^{n} r^2 = \tfrac{1}{6}n(n+1)(2n+1); \quad \sum_{r=1}^{n} r^3 = \tfrac{1}{4}n^2(n+1)^2$$

- You can use the standard formulae above for $\sum_{r=1}^{n} r, \sum_{r=1}^{n} r^2$ and $\sum_{r=1}^{n} r^3$ to find formulae for other summations as follows.

$$\sum_{r=1}^{n} (ar^3 + br^2 + cr + d) = a\sum_{r=1}^{n} r^3 + b\sum_{r=1}^{n} r^2 + c\sum_{r=1}^{n} r + dn$$

Using standard summation formulae to find formulae for more complicated summations

Suppose you are asked to find a formula for $\sum_{r=1}^{n} (3r^2 + r + 4)$. This will be an expression in terms of n which gives you the total of the sum for any value of n. For example, if you substitute $n = 100$ into this expression, you will get the value of $\sum_{r=1}^{100} (3r^2 + r + 4)$ straightaway, without having to calculate and sum all one hundred terms. One way to find the formula is to consider the summation written out term by term as follows.

$$\sum_{r=1}^{n}(3r^2 + r + 4) = \begin{aligned}&(3 \times 1^2 &+ &1 &+ &4) \\ +\ &(3 \times 2^2 &+ &2 &+ &4) \\ +\ &(3 \times 3^2 &+ &3 &+ &4) \\ +\ &\dots \\ +\ &(3 \times n^2 &+ &n &+ &4)\end{aligned}$$

Second column

First column

Third column

The sum of the terms in the first column is the same as $3\sum_{r=1}^{n}r^2$. The sum

of the terms in the second column is the same as $\sum_{r=1}^{n}r$. The last column

is n lots of 4 which equals $4n$.

You can split the summation you were given like this and then use the

standard formulae $\sum_{r=1}^{n}r = \frac{1}{2}n(n+1)$ and $\sum_{r=1}^{n}r^2 = \frac{1}{6}n(n+1)(2n+1)$ to

get the answer as follows:

$$\sum_{r=1}^{n}(3r^2 + r + 4) = 3\sum_{r=1}^{n}r^2 + \sum_{r=1}^{n}r + 4n$$

$$= 3 \times \tfrac{1}{6}n(n+1)(2n+1) + \tfrac{1}{2}n(n+1) + 4n$$

Taking out $\frac{1}{2}$ as a common factor.

$$= \tfrac{1}{2}(n(n+1)(2n+1) + n(n+1) + 8n)$$

Taking out n as a common factor.

$$= \tfrac{1}{2}n((n+1)(2n+1) + (n+1) + 8)$$

$$= \tfrac{1}{2}n(2n^2 + 4n + 10)$$

$$= n(n^2 + 2n + 5)$$

EXAMPLE 1

Find $\sum_{r=1}^{n}3r(r-1)$, expressing your answer in a fully factorised form.

SOLUTION

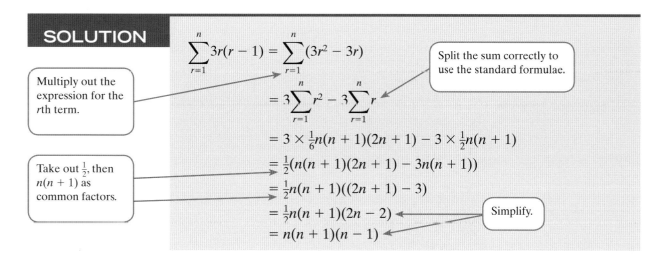

Multiply out the expression for the rth term.

$$\sum_{r=1}^{n}3r(r-1) = \sum_{r=1}^{n}(3r^2 - 3r)$$

Split the sum correctly to use the standard formulae.

$$= 3\sum_{r=1}^{n}r^2 - 3\sum_{r=1}^{n}r$$

Take out $\frac{1}{2}$, then $n(n+1)$ as common factors.

$$= 3 \times \tfrac{1}{6}n(n+1)(2n+1) - 3 \times \tfrac{1}{2}n(n+1)$$

$$= \tfrac{1}{2}(n(n+1)(2n+1) - 3n(n+1))$$

$$= \tfrac{1}{2}n(n+1)((2n+1) - 3)$$

$$= \tfrac{1}{2}n(n+1)(2n-2)$$

Simplify.

$$= n(n+1)(n-1)$$

EXAMPLE 2

Use the standard formulae for $\sum_{r=1}^{n}r$, $\sum_{r=1}^{n}r^2$ and $\sum_{r=1}^{n}r^3$ to calculate the

value of

$$1 \times 2 \times 3 + 2 \times 3 \times 4 + 3 \times 4 \times 5 + \dots + 49 \times 50 \times 51$$

SOLUTION

Be careful with this value. It is the value of r that gives the last term in the sum.

Expressing the sum in sigma notation gives

$$1 \times 2 \times 3 + 2 \times 3 \times 4 + 3 \times 4 \times 5 + \ldots + 49 \times 50 \times 51$$

$$= \sum_{r=1}^{49} r(r+1)(r+2)$$

Check that substituting $r = 1$ gives the first term, $r = 2$ gives the second term, etc.

Now

$$\sum_{r=1}^{49} r(r+1)(r+2) = \sum_{r=1}^{49} (r^3 + 3r^2 + 2r)$$

$$= \sum_{r=1}^{49} r^3 + 3\sum_{r=1}^{49} r^2 + 2\sum_{r=1}^{49} r$$

To work out the values of $\sum_{r=1}^{49} r^3$, $\sum_{r=1}^{49} r^2$ and $\sum_{r=1}^{49} r$ just substitute $n = 49$ into the corresponding standard formulae, which are:

$$\sum_{r=1}^{n} r^3 = \tfrac{1}{4}n^2(n+1)^2, \quad \sum_{r=1}^{n} r^2 = \tfrac{1}{6}n(n+1)(2n+1) \quad \text{and} \quad \sum_{r=1}^{n} r = \tfrac{1}{2}n(n+1).$$

This gives $1\,500\,625$, $40\,425$ and 1225. So the final answer is

$$1\,500\,625 + 3 \times 40\,425 + 2 \times 1225 = 1\,624\,350.$$

2 The method of differences

K KEY FACTS

- The method of differences involves writing each term in a given summation as an expression involving subtraction. This leads to lots of cancellation. What remains is an algebraic formula for the summation, as shown in the following example.

Since $\dfrac{1}{r(r+1)} \equiv \dfrac{1}{r} - \dfrac{1}{r+1}$,

$$\sum_{r=1}^{n} \frac{1}{r(r+1)} = \sum_{r=1}^{n} \left(\frac{1}{r} - \frac{1}{r+1} \right)$$

$$= \left(\frac{1}{1} - \frac{1}{2} \right) + \left(\frac{1}{2} - \frac{1}{3} \right) + \left(\frac{1}{3} - \frac{1}{4} \right) + \ldots + \left(\frac{1}{n-2} - \frac{1}{n-1} \right) + \left(\frac{1}{n-1} - \frac{1}{n} \right) + \left(\frac{1}{n} - \frac{1}{n+1} \right)$$

$$= \frac{1}{1} - \frac{1}{2} + \frac{1}{2} - \frac{1}{3} - \frac{1}{4} + \ldots + \frac{1}{n-2} - \frac{1}{n-1} - \frac{1}{n} + \frac{1}{n} - \frac{1}{n+1}$$

$$= 1 - \frac{1}{n+1}$$

Using algebraic identities and the method of differences to find formulae for summations

The identity $\dfrac{1}{r^3} - \dfrac{1}{(r+1)^3} \equiv \dfrac{(r+1)^3 - r^3}{r^3(r+1)^3} \equiv \dfrac{3r^2 + 3r + 1}{r^3(r+1)^3}$ can be

used to find a formula for $\displaystyle\sum_{r=1}^{n} \frac{3r^2 + 3r + 1}{r^3(r+1)^3}$ as follows.

$$\sum_{r=1}^{n} \frac{3r^2 + 3r + 1}{r^3(r+1)^3} \equiv \sum_{r=1}^{n}\left(\frac{1}{r^3} - \frac{1}{(r+1)^3}\right)$$

> Here you use the identity mentioned above.

> Here it is best to write out the first and last three terms in full, to help you see the pattern of cancelling.

$$= \left[\frac{1}{1^3} - \frac{1}{2^3}\right] + \left[\frac{1}{2^3} - \frac{1}{3^3}\right] + \left[\frac{1}{3^3} - \frac{1}{4^3}\right]$$

$$+ \dots + \left[\frac{1}{(n-2)^3} - \frac{1}{(n-1)^3}\right] + \left[\frac{1}{(n-1)^3} - \frac{1}{n^3}\right] + \left[\frac{1}{n^3} - \frac{1}{(n+1)^3}\right]$$

$$= \frac{1}{1^3} - \frac{1}{2^3} + \frac{1}{2^3} - \frac{1}{3^3} + \frac{1}{3^3} - \frac{1}{4^3}$$

$$+ \dots + \frac{1}{(n-2)^3} - \frac{1}{(n-1)^3} + \frac{1}{(n-1)^3} - \frac{1}{n^3} + \frac{1}{n^3} - \frac{1}{(n+1)^3}$$

$$= 1 - \frac{1}{(n+1)^3}$$

EXAMPLE 3

Show that $\dfrac{1}{r+1} - \dfrac{1}{r+2} \equiv \dfrac{1}{(r+1)(r+2)}$. Hence use the method of

differences to find the sum of the series $\displaystyle\sum_{r=1}^{n} \frac{1}{(r+1)(r+2)}$.

SOLUTION

$$\frac{1}{r+1} - \frac{1}{r+2} \equiv \frac{(r+2) - (r+1)}{(r+1)(r+2)} \equiv \frac{1}{(r+1)(r+2)}$$

> Express as a single fraction over a common denominator.

$$\sum_{r=1}^{n} \frac{1}{(r+1)(r+2)} \equiv \sum_{r=1}^{n}\left[\frac{1}{(r+1)} - \frac{1}{(r+2)}\right]$$

> Use the identity that you've already proved.

> Write out the summation 'in full' (at least the first three terms and the last three terms); be careful to get the value of r correct in each case.

$$= \left[\frac{1}{2} - \frac{1}{3}\right] + \left[\frac{1}{3} - \frac{1}{4}\right] + \left[\frac{1}{4} - \frac{1}{5}\right] + \left[\frac{1}{5} - \frac{1}{6}\right] + \dots$$

$$+ \left[\frac{1}{n-2} - \frac{1}{n-1}\right] + \left[\frac{1}{n-1} - \frac{1}{n}\right] + \left[\frac{1}{n} - \frac{1}{n+1}\right] +$$

$$\left[\frac{1}{n+1} - \frac{1}{n+2}\right]$$

$$= \frac{1}{2} - \frac{1}{n+2}$$

> Cancel groups of items within terms that add up to zero in the sum. These will occur throughout the sum in a pattern. In this example only the first and last items don't cancel.

EXAMPLE 4

You are given that $\dfrac{2}{r(r+1)(r+2)} \equiv \dfrac{1}{r} - \dfrac{2}{r+1} + \dfrac{1}{r+2}$.

Use the method of differences to show that

$$\sum_{r=1}^{n} \frac{2}{r(r+1)(r+2)} = \frac{1}{2} - \frac{1}{(n+1)(n+2)}.$$

Hence find the sum of the infinite series

$$\frac{1}{1 \times 2 \times 3} + \frac{1}{2 \times 3 \times 4} + \frac{1}{3 \times 4 \times 5} + \dots.$$

SOLUTION

$$\sum_{r=1}^{n} \frac{2}{r(r + 1)(r + 2)}$$

> Use the information you were given,
> $$\frac{2}{r(r + 1)(r + 2)} \equiv \frac{1}{r} - \frac{2}{r + 1} + \frac{1}{r + 2}.$$
> This gives you a different way of expressing the rth term in the series, which allows you to use the method of differences.

$$= \sum_{r=1}^{n} \left[\frac{1}{r} - \frac{2}{r + 1} + \frac{1}{r + 2}\right]$$

$$= \left[\frac{1}{1} - \frac{2}{2} + \frac{1}{3}\right] +$$

$$\left[\frac{1}{2} - \frac{2}{3} + \frac{1}{4}\right] +$$

> Write out the sum in full. Be careful to get the value of r correct in each case. Because there are three algebraic fractions in the sum, four terms at the start and end of the sum have been included; this will make it easier to spot the pattern of cancellation.

$$\left[\frac{1}{3} - \frac{2}{4} + \frac{1}{5}\right] +$$

$$\left[\frac{1}{4} - \frac{2}{5} + \frac{1}{6}\right] + \ldots$$

> The terms have been written below one another, offset so that the groups that add up to zero appear in vertical columns. You might find this technique helps you too, but it doesn't apply to all sums so be careful.

$$\ldots + \left[\frac{1}{n - 3} - \frac{2}{n - 2} + \frac{1}{n - 1}\right]$$

$$+ \left[\frac{1}{n - 2} - \frac{2}{n - 1} + \frac{1}{n}\right]$$

$$+ \left[\frac{1}{n - 1} - \frac{2}{n} + \frac{1}{n + 1}\right]$$

$$+ \left[\frac{1}{n} - \frac{2}{n + 1} + \frac{1}{n + 2}\right]$$

$$= \frac{1}{1} - \frac{2}{2} + \frac{1}{2} + \frac{1}{n + 1} - \frac{2}{n + 1} + \frac{1}{n + 2} = \frac{1}{2} - \frac{1}{n + 1} + \frac{1}{n + 2}$$

$$= \frac{1}{2} + \frac{(n + 1) - (n + 2)}{(n + 1)(n + 2)}$$

> As n tends to infinity, $\frac{1}{2} - \frac{1}{(n + 1)(n + 2)}$ tends to $\frac{1}{2}$, since $\frac{1}{(n + 1)(n + 2)}$ tends to 0 as n increases.

$$= \frac{1}{2} - \frac{1}{(n + 1)(n + 2)}$$

Hence the sum of the infinite series

$$\frac{1}{1 \times 2 \times 3} + \frac{1}{2 \times 3 \times 4} + \frac{1}{3 \times 4 \times 5} + \ldots \text{ is } \frac{1}{2}.$$

LINKS
Pure Mathematics   C2

Test Yourself

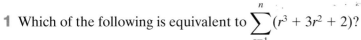

1 Which of the following is equivalent to $\sum_{r=1}^{n}(r^3 + 3r^2 + 2)$?

A $\sum_{r=1}^{n} r^3 + \sum_{r=1}^{n} r^2 + 2n$

B $\sum_{r=1}^{n} r^3 + 3\sum_{r=1}^{n} r^2 + 2$

C $\sum_{r=1}^{n} r^3 + 3\sum_{r=1}^{n} r^2 + 2n$

D $n^3 + 3n^2 + 2$

2 Which of the following represents the first n terms of $(2 \times 5) + (3 \times 7) + (4 \times 9) + \dots$ expressed in sigma notation?

   A $\displaystyle\sum_{r=1}^{n}(r + 1)(2r + 3)$ **B** $\displaystyle\sum_{r=1}^{n}(r + 1)(r + 4)$ **C** $\displaystyle\sum_{r=1}^{n}2r(r + 4)$ **D** $\displaystyle\sum_{r=1}^{n}2r(2r + 3)$

3 Use the method of differences to find the value of $\displaystyle\sum_{r=1}^{10}[(r + 1)^2 - r^2]$.

   A 121   **B** 120   **C** −121   **D** −120

4 Find a formula, in terms of n, for $\displaystyle\sum_{r=1}^{n}\left[\dfrac{1}{(r + 1)^2} - \dfrac{1}{(r + 2)^2}\right]$.

   A $\dfrac{1}{2} - \dfrac{1}{(n + 2)^2}$ **B** $\dfrac{1}{(n + 1)^2} - \dfrac{1}{(n + 2)^2}$ **C** $1 - \dfrac{1}{(n + 2)^2}$ **D** $\dfrac{1}{4} - \dfrac{1}{(n + 2)^2}$

5 The sum of the first n odd numbers can be written as $\displaystyle\sum_{r=1}^{n}(2r - 1)$. Using the standard formulae, which of the following is a fully simplified formula for this?

   A $n^2 + n - 1$ **B** $n(n + 2)$ **C** n^2 **D** $\frac{1}{3}n(2n - 1)(n + 2)$

Exam-Style Question

Using the identity $\dfrac{5r + 2}{r(r + 1)(r + 2)} \equiv \dfrac{1}{r} + \dfrac{3}{r + 1} - \dfrac{4}{r + 2}$, find a formula for $\displaystyle\sum_{r=1}^{n}\dfrac{5r + 2}{r(r + 1)(r + 2)}$.

Hence find the value of $\displaystyle\sum_{r=1}^{\infty}\dfrac{5r + 2}{r(r + 1)(r + 2)}$.

Index

Formulae and results

Finite series

$$\sum_{r=1}^{n} r = \tfrac{1}{2}n(n+1) \qquad \sum_{r=1}^{n} r^2 = \tfrac{1}{6}n(n+1)(2n+1) \qquad \sum_{r=1}^{n} r^3 = \tfrac{1}{4}n^2(n+1)^2$$

Equations

If $ax^3 + bx^2 + cx + d = 0$ has roots α, β, γ then

$$\alpha + \beta + \gamma = \frac{-b}{a}, \; \beta\gamma + \alpha\gamma + \alpha\beta = \frac{c}{a}, \; \alpha\beta\gamma = \frac{-b}{a}, \; a \neq 0$$

Complex numbers

Cartesian form

$z = x + jy$ (The notation is also used.)

$\text{Re}(z) = x; \qquad \text{Im}(z) = y.$

$\text{mod } z = |z| = \sqrt{(x^2 + y^2)}.$

$\arg z = \theta$

where $\cos\theta = \dfrac{x}{|z|}$ and $\sin\theta = \dfrac{y}{|z|}$ and $-\pi < \theta \leqslant \pi$

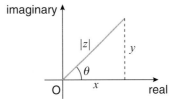

(arg 0 is undefined)

Conjugate of z, $z^* = x - jy$. (The notation $\bar{z}$ is also used.)

$$zz^* = |z|^2, \frac{1}{z} = \frac{x - jy}{x^2 + y^2} = \frac{z^*}{|z|^2}$$

Modulus-argument (polar) form

If $|z| = r$ and $\arg z = \theta$, then $z = [r, \theta] = r(\cos\theta + j\sin\theta)$

$z^* = r(\cos\theta - j\sin\theta), \dfrac{1}{z} = \dfrac{1}{r}(\cos\theta - j\sin\theta)$